AGGERS'
SPECIAL DELIVERY

Trivial Delights from the World of Cricket

Printed and bound in Great Britain by MPG Books Ltd, Bodmin

Published by Sanctuary Publishing Limited, Sanctuary House,
45–53 Sinclair Road, London W14 0NS, United Kingdom

www.sanctuarypublishing.com

Cover: Ash
Illustrations: BrindeauMexter

ISBN: 1-86074-630-6

AGGERS'
SPECIAL DELIVERY
Trivial Delights from the World of Cricket

Jonathan Agnew with Nick Constable

arcane

— FOREWORD —

Devotees of BBC Radio 4's *Test Match Special* are already aware that the great game of cricket is far more than merely a spectator sport. During every match, cricket, with its deep and fascinating history, produces an avalanche of statistics and a treasure trove of colourful memories and stories – at least some of which are true. Lump this bewildering mass of information together, and you have cricketing trivia. At least, that's what a commentator might call it.

Put this to a statistician, however, and one is asking for trouble. Bill Frindall, the 'Bearded Wonder', will snort dismissively at any suggestion that his overnight research into the records of lower-order wicket-keeping left-handed batsmen playing at the Oval since the Second World War is, in fact, nothing but trivia. His punishment will be to conceal the bowling figures from the offending commentator for at least the following half hour. In that situation, my revenge is to concede that his hard work the previous night was, indeed, admirable, and that I had just heard a rumour from the television statistician (that really upsets him!) that we are on the verge of the record for the number of threes that have been scored in this series. In order to underline his reputation as the finest 'notcher' in the land, can he please check? Immediately?

The arrival of email to *Test Match Special* has opened a whole new world of opportunity for fans of cricket trivia. Hitting the screen of a rather elderly laptop at the back of the box at an alarming rate, this can take either of two forms. Firstly, it can be a question from a listener – something along the lines of 'Can the commentators tell me the last time a batsman hit five consecutive fours in a test match? From Dave in Watford.'

Secondly, it can be a response to a challenge from a commentator, often during a dull passage of play: 'Let us know your most unusual example of play being interrupted.' My favourite answer from the thousands submitted to that request, incidentally – apart from mid-on exploding (the only cricket-playing casualty in wartime) – was a mole burrowing through the surface of the pitch in the middle of a game! Oh, to have been there!

It is a surprising fact that many top-level cricketers display little interest in stats or cricket trivia, even when it concerns them directly. 'Have you ever been out first ball?' I once asked the former New Zealand captain Jeremy Coney while touting for new members of the Primary Club. 'No,' he responded defiantly, thereby avoiding the need to pay up. It took only a few minutes for the first email to arrive, setting out the precise date and location when Coney had indeed been dismissed first ball. By the next morning we were armed with no fewer than four separate and verified instances of Coney falling first ball in first-class cricket!

This book will not answer questions like that. But, thanks to the exhaustive research of Nick Constable – for which I am extremely grateful – it forms an essential accompaniment to a day of either watching or listening to cricket. It will make you smile. It will raise your eyebrows. It might even inspire you to join our formidable and tireless band of trivia emailers to *TMS*. Just don't always expect the right answer, that's all!

Jonathan Agnew
February 2005

— INTRODUCTION —

First, a technical point about cricket trivia. Jonathan has already alluded to the dangers of describing cricket scorers and statistical archivists as trivia-merchants. Quite right too. That fiercely independent and dedicated band of brethren are guardians of the game's history. They would rather die horribly in a vat of boiling sweat harvested from the armpits of the Barmy Army than spill a drop of cocoa onto the 'Fielding Extras' column.

But we cricket trivialists also represent a proud and noble tradition, one that reaches beyond mere number crunching and into the game's *spirit*. This, of course, is the crucial technical difference between us and them. To give just one example; in the spring of 1994 Orange Free State played the touring Australians in a four-day match at Springbok Park, Bloemfontein. The scorecard states that Australia won by 60 runs, despite Hansie Cronje's 251, and that Merv Hughes returned bowling figures of 25-2-127-4 including one wide in the second innings.

What it won't tell you – but we will on page 166 – is why play was suspended for three minutes following a Hughes ball which caused the on-strike Cronje to collapse in helpless laughter and the fielding Aussies to suffer collective hysteria. You could never record this incident properly on the card – not even in the Bowling Extras column – yet it's typical of the high jinks, japes and jollity that infuse cricket at every level. This is the kind of stuff we trivialists adore…and what *Aggers' Special Delivery* is all about.

In years to come, when sports science degree students are handed this tome as a key textbook, some may wonder what a former England fast bowler and highly-respected BBC sports broadcaster had in common with a hack writer who trundles in for Lynton 2nds in the North Devon Holiday Homes League (Division 5). The answer of course is simple: A shared, deep affection for the greatest game on God's earth.

If you don't like cricket trivia stop now. What follows could do your head in.

Nick Constable
February 2005

— TEN WAYS TO GET OUT —

Bowled
Caught
Run out
Stumped
Hit wicket
Leg before wicket
Handled the ball
Double hit
Timed out
Obstructing the field

The first five are all-too familiar to your average club cricketer. LBW is a different kettle of haddock altogether – akin to the confusion over football's offside rule – but you'll find a handy bluffers' guide to this law, complete with diagrams, elsewhere on these pages.

That leaves the last four outs, guaranteed to provide healthy (if slurred) late-night debate among members of cricket tour parties. Here's the Agnew guide to being a smug know-it-all.

- **Handled the Ball:** A batsman can be out if, after playing a shot, he or she uses a hand to knock the ball clear of the stumps. Fielders appeal in the usual way. Michael Vaughan, no less, has been given out like this in a Test match, against India. (Note: It's bad form to appeal if a batsman is merely picking the ball up to save fielders the trouble.)

- **Double Hit:** It's extremely rare, but you can be given out if you attempt a second strike at a delivery with the intention of scoring runs. Defending a wicket with your bat or assisting fielders doesn't count.

- **Timed Out:** Technically speaking, you can be out even before you're in. Batsmen must be ready to face a ball within three minutes of the previous wicket falling. Fielders who try this appeal are just too jolly unsporting for words. Then again…

- **Obstructing the Field:** Batsmen who deliberately foil a run-out or catch by barging or impeding an opponent can face the Long Walk. This is perhaps an obvious candidate for a third-umpire decision, but it's so unusual that TV producers could die waiting for it to happen.

— MASSAGE PARLEY —

In the good old days, when bowlers trained on fried breakfasts and Australian teams were fallible, talk of a massage in the dressing room would have attracted funny looks. But now that science is the Great God of international sport, cricketers want their pound of flesh properly pummelled.

So as England prepared for their 2004 trip to the West Indies, skipper Michael Vaughan was confident his ECB bosses would fork out for a tour masseuse – specifically the talented Vicki Byrne, who has a reputation for rubbing down sport's finest. Vaughan pointed out that the country's rugby team had employed a masseur during its World Cup triumph and the same service was crucial if England's fast bowlers were to stay fit on rock-hard Windies wickets.

Sadly, times at the ECB are equally hard. Vaughan was told that the Board would cough up one-third of the cost, while a sponsor would provide another third and the players could jolly well pay the rest. A player revolt would therefore have signalled the delightful prospect of Byrne manipulating Steve Harmison's hamstring, donning a sponsor's shirt to do his back and leaving the rest to him.

The ECB insisted that it had agreed to pay for a masseur 'sourced locally' in the West Indies. A spokesman added, 'Vikki worked for the team throughout last summer and the players wanted her on board for this tour as part of the management team. While we want to give the England players the best possible support, we have had to operate within certain financial constraints during the last year and we can't throw money at the team.'

Fortunately, a deal was struck. Byrne joined the party, England won their first Test Series in the West Indies for 36 years (3-0) and a super-fit Harmison reminded the Windies what quick bowling is all about.

— SACHIN TON-DULKAR —

The most prolific batsmen in one-day-international history is India's Sachin Tendulkar, regarded as having almost god-like status in his home city of Mumbai. Tendulkar made his debut in 1989, then just 16, and within 15 years had 37 hundreds to his name.

— QUACKING UP —

West Indian cricketer Laurie Johnson was already depressed after being out first ball while playing for Derbyshire against Sussex at Queen's Park, Chesterfield. Things got worse in the second innings when he again succumbed to his first delivery. Trudging off with a golden duck to his name, he must have wondered whether he'd somehow upset the Almighty. Especially when a pair of ducks from the adjoining lake landed on the pitch and followed him off.

— CUTTING EDGE —

It may stick in the craw of cricket traditionalists but the game is embracing computer technology as never before. Perhaps the best-known system is Hawk-Eye, a computer graphics package which predicts the path of a ball after it hits a batsman's pad. This allows TV viewers to see in seconds whether or not an lbw decision is correct.

Hawk-Eye, invented by scientist Paul Hawkins, works by tracking a ball from the moment it leaves a bowler's hand, using six TV cameras set up at different angles around the pitch. Since its introduction in 2001, it has revolutionised Test cricket coverage, allowing analysts – and players – to see the trajectory of every ball bowled.

Logically, it was only a matter of time before Hawk-Eye moved into the coaching business, and the potential for international cricketers is now mind-blowing. Using virtual-reality goggles and a bat wired to computers, it's possible to see, say, Sri Lanka's Muttiah Muralitharan running in to bowl a repeat of one of his *actual* Test-match spells. The merciless software then delivers a report showing whether the batsman hit boundaries, nicked edges or got clean bowled.

'In the future, I see no reason why it will not be realistic enough that international batsmen – particularly in one-day cricket – will wear the headset while waiting to come in to bat so that, when they get to the wicket, they will already have their eye in,' says Hawk-Eye inventor Paul Hawkins. Er, maybe. Batsmen who've spent 20 minutes being bamboozled by a virtual Murali in the dressing room may develop an unexplained wrist injury by the time they have to face the genuine article.

— AGE TRAP —

It's tough being a living legend. Sir Isaac Vivian Alexander Richards tells how, at his peak, it seemed bowlers were sending down basketballs, so easy were they to hit. Later on, the same bowlers appeared to be using marbles. Now the balls look like peas. 'I can't see 'em and I can't hit 'em,' bemoans Sir Viv.

Age may have wearied him, but time can't touch the scorebooks. In 121 Tests he made 8,540 runs at an average of 50.23, including 24 centuries (his top score was 291 against England). He remains the only West Indian captain never to have lost a Test series and he still holds the record for the fastest Test century – just 56 balls.

However, the abiding curse of greatness is that everyone wants to take you on, particularly lithe young prodigies seeking a prestigious scalp. 'I'm past 50, for heaven's sake,' says Sir Viv. 'They'll still be trying to get me out in 40 years. "Hey, I got Viv out yesterday," they'll say. "Hey, well done. I'm 90 and I'm in a wheelchair," I'll say back. "Give me a break."'

— ALEC'S JAFFA —

Given that Sir Donald Bradman was – and remains – the best batsman in Test history, Alec Bedser must have been chuffed to bowl him for 0 at Adelaide in the 1946/7 Ashes series. Alec's grin must have become semi-permanent on hearing Bradman's typically generous after-match comment. 'It was the best ball I've ever faced,' he said.

— SLEDGE ARTISTES —

Australians are seen as the kings of 'sledge' – cricket jargon for verbally winding up opponents – but in truth this has long been part of the first-class game in all the Test nations. One classic joust came in the 1974/5 Ashes series when Tony Greig arrived in Australia with the declared intention of goading Dennis Lillee, arguably the most fearsome Aussie quick ever to breathe fire.

In the first test at Brisbane, Greig, a fast-medium all-rounder, greeted Lillee with a string of short-pitched balls, eventually bouncing him out. Livid Lillee stormed into the dressing room and announced ominously to his team-mates, 'Just remember who started this thing. But we'll finish it.' Unfortunately, even the great Lillee had found a worthy opponent in Greig, who laughed at his threats, dodged his bouncers like a shadow boxer and regularly despatched him to the boundary with observations such as, 'That's four, Dennis. Fetch that!'

The strategy worked well for Greig, who not only smashed a flamboyant 110 in the game but also went on to notch a respectable series average of 40.54, taking 17 wickets and 12 catches in the process. While he could look after himself against Lillee and some new kid called Jeff Thomson, the rest of the England batsmen weren't quite up for the crack. In fact, most of the cracks came from their bones under an onslaught of Thommo bouncers. Young Jeff took nine wickets in the match and 33 in the series to secure a 4–1 win for the home side. The only Test England won was the last, in which Lillee was injured and Thomson absent.

Unfortunately for Greig, the upfront approach didn't always come off. Before England's 1976 home Test against the West Indies, he indulged in a bit of mass-sledging, loftily pronouncing, 'I intend to make them grovel.' Perhaps he was referring to his own team-mates, and, if so, the Windies duly obliged. England were pounded into oblivion courtesy of Vanburn Holder, Wayne Daniel, Andy Roberts and a youthful Michael Holding (cheerily – and understandably – nicknamed Whispering Death by fans). In the final Oval Test, Holding's breathtaking speed saw half of England's wickets fall for 78 to give him figures of 20.5-6-57-6 and 14 for 149 in the match.

As Greig learned, best to think before you sledge. My BBC colleague and former England fast bowler Angus Fraser recalls bowling to Aussie skipper Allan Border when, after one delivery, Border barked, 'Faced better bowlers than you, mate.' Angus was *about* to respond, 'And I've bowled at better batsman.' However, he kept schtum, realising that, actually, he hadn't. It was a wise call. His next ball went for six.

Perhaps best known of all sledging tales in the English county game is the confrontation between fiery England and Glamorgan fast bowler Greg Thomas and Viv Richards. Thomas had just bowled a magnificent outswinger that Richards missed outside off stump. 'It's red, it's round and it weighs about five ounces,' fumed Thomas. 'Now, try to hit it.' Richards obliged by putting his next ball out of the ground. Then he sauntered nonchalantly down the pitch, prodding at imaginary bumps, until he was within earshot. 'Greg, you know what it looks like,' said the great man. 'Now go and find it.'

— BACK TO SCHOOL —

After years of umming and aahing, a campaign for UK state schools to embrace cricket as part of the PE curriculum is finally under way. The Cricket Foundation – led by the governor of the Bank of England, Mervyn King, and former Worcestershire chairman Duncan Fearnley – is seeking to increase the number of schools offering competitive matches. Currently, only a third of state secondaries and a quarter of primaries get involved.

The emphasis on state schools is seen as crucial if the English game is to ditch its lingering image as a posh sport. Anyone who seriously doubts that elitism persists should consider the number of privately educated cricketers playing the first-class game – around two in every five. The number of British children educated privately is less than one in ten.

— SHORT SHIFT —

The Association of Cricket Umpires and Scorers had a particular need for larger recruits at the end of the 2004 season after its entire stock of small-size umpire jackets was stolen from a garage in Rainham, Kent. Quite how the burglars planned to dispose of their haul is unclear, but ice-cream vendors of short stature may be looking unusually dapper.

— SHRINKING PITCH —

As if playing cricket isn't hard enough. The annual beach match between the Royal Southern Yacht Club of Hamble, Hampshire, and the Island Sailing Club of the Isle of Wight is being threatened by rising sea levels, blamed on global warming and the gradual sinking of southern England.

For more than 50 years, players have sailed out to a sandbank in the middle of the Solent, 200 yards of which is exposed once a year by exceptionally low spring tides. Unfortunately, it's getting less exposed by the year, with the result that the usual 40-minute challenge – billed as the shortest cricket match in the world – will soon become a half-hour thrash that makes 20–20 look Boycottian in comparison! Who knows? Warmer seas may even bring more sharks into British waters. It'll be a brave skipper who slows the over rate!

— BOWLING GIANTS —

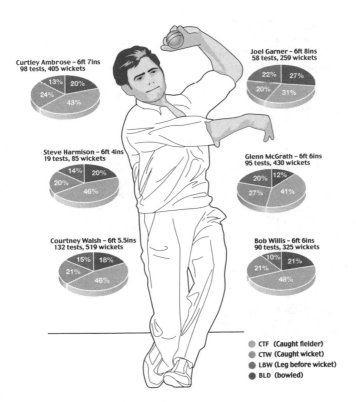

Curtley Ambrose – 6ft 7ins
98 tests, 405 wickets
13% | 20% | 24% | 43%

Joel Garner – 6ft 8ins
58 tests, 259 wickets
22% | 27% | 20% | 31%

Steve Harmison – 6ft 4ins
19 tests, 85 wickets
14% | 20% | 20% | 46%

Glenn McGrath – 6ft 6ins
95 tests, 430 wickets
20% | 12% | 27% | 41%

Courtney Walsh – 6ft 5.5ins
132 tests, 519 wickets
15% | 18% | 21% | 46%

Bob Willis – 6ft 6ins
90 tests, 325 wickets
10% | 21% | 21% | 48%

● CTF (Caught fielder)
● CTW (Caught wicket)
● LBW (Leg before wicket)
● BLD (bowled)

— GROUNDSMAN'S LOT —

Most club cricketers have, at some time, batted on strips that appear to have been recently strafed by an Apache attack helicopter. This can be disconcerting if the ground is hard and the opposition's quick bowler, fuelled by five pints of Gutwarbler Special at lunchtime, is coming off his long run.

Respect is due, then, to the ECB, which has bankrolled Cranfield University's new course on 'wicket performance'. According to the literature, the uni's Centre for Sports Surfaces will 'investigate the principles between rolling intensity, duration and contact pressure and the initial soil water status of cricket pitches in order to optimise playing performance and enhance safety'. And you thought 'ground-keeping' meant leaning on the heavy roller for a smoke.

— HARMY HIGHS —

As England's first seriously quick paceman since Bob Willis, Steve Harmison's broad shoulders carry a heavy load. There have been plenty of false dawns for England fast bowlers over the years, but this time the hype is matched by the sight of hopping batsmen and cartwheeling wickets. Here's how Harmy has emerged as one of the world's most feared strike bowlers.

1996	Makes debut for Durham County Cricket Club.
2000	Selected for England squad.
2002	Full Test debut against India at Trent Bridge.
2002	Tough overseas baptism in Ashes tour.
2003	Returns from Bangladesh with spine injury.
2003	Begins rigorous training programme with Newcastle United FC.
2004	Takes 23 wickets in the Caribbean Tests.
2004	Takes 21 wickets in the 3–0 home win against New Zealand.

And a breakdown of Harmison's rise and rise in PriceWaterhouseCoopers world rankings:

Date	Position
August 2002	67th
December 2002	56th
January 2003	30th
October 2003	19th
March 2004	9th
June 2004	2nd
August 2004	1st

— OVAL CURSE —

English batsmen playing one-day internationals at The Oval need to take particular care if they reach the brink of a century. Andrew Flintoff (vs India, 2004) is one of four players to be out on 99 at this ground. The others are Geoff Boycott (who, incidentally, was the first player in ODI history to fall on 99) in 1980, Allan Lamb in 1982 and Chris Broad in 1987.

— SUNNY OUTLOOK —

Cricket lovers are always ready to debate a batsman's Test record but sometimes forget the standard of bowling faced. This is why the sublime Indian opener Sunil 'Sunny' Gavaskar stands out among the game's giants – not just for his 10,122 Test runs (average 51.12), nor his unique record of scoring centuries in each innings three times, nor even his record number of Test centuries (34). What really elevates Gavaskar to the pantheon of batting greats is the quality of his opponents.

The first of two great batting feats came during his 1971 Test debut, when he smashed the Indian record for most runs in a series, posting 774 against the West Indies. The second was his country's highest individual innings in a Test Match: 236 not out at Madras during the Windies' 1983/4 tour. Do we spot a theme emerging here? It was an era that saw Gavaskar facing the most fearsome battery of fast bowlers ever seen in world cricket: Andy Roberts, Colin Croft, Joel Garner, Malcolm Marshall and Michael Holding. Just typing their names makes you nervous. Gavaskar saw them all. And saw them off.

— RUN HAPPY —

Love 'em or loathe 'em, no one can doubt the role the Aussies have played in revitalising Test cricket. The table below shows, decade by decade, the average number of runs scored per over and compares Australia's progress with that of England. You'll see that Australia increased its run rate by an average 33 per cent over the last two decades of the 20th century and by 2000 had reached 3.81 per over – 0.7 faster than their nearest rival, Sri Lanka, and the highest return in cricket history.

Over the same two decades, England's run rate rose by around 14 per cent to 3.1 – roughly the same as South Africa, Pakistan and India. The West Indies were just under the 3.0 mark, while New Zealand stood slightly above 2.8.

Decade beginning	England	Australia
1870	2.7	2.2
1880	2.5	2.3
1890	2.7	2.6
1900	2.7	3.1
1910	2.9	3.4
1920	2.7	2.7
1930	2.7	3.0
1940	2.4	2.9
1950	2.3	2.5
1960	2.5	2.6
1970	2.5	2.7
1980	2.8	2.8
1990	2.9	3.2
2000	3.1	3.8

— ZENMEYANG UMPIRE? —

In a tireless search for top-quality and magnificently useless cricketing trivia, we can reveal that the familiar 'howzat?' lbw appeal translates as 'zenmeyang' in Chinese Mandarin. A little something is lost in translation – *zenmeyang* is actually a polite enquiry about a person's general wellbeing – but it'll have to do.

We mention this only because the Chinese government is massively in favour of cricket and when they're in favour of something they don't muck about. In the 1960s it was decided that the country should take up athletics and swimming virtually from scratch. They might as well have turned a giant Hoover on the International Olympic Committee medal factory. It was pretty much the same with chess. China recently came from nowhere to produce two women world champions: Xie Jun and Zhu Chen.

Schools in Beijing, Shanghai and Guangzhou have been instructed to teach cricket (known as *ban qiu* in Mandarin) from 2005, and a ground in Beijing has been pencilled in as an international venue. Apparently, the game appeals to the Chinese leadership because they believe it combines strategic thinking and quick responses. So they've obviously never been on tour to the West Country.

The government's target is to play a World Cup tournament within 15 years and a full Test within 20. While expatriates are still the backbone of the game, Chinese players have competed in international tournaments at the Shanghai Cricket Club since 1994. China has also turned to neighbouring countries for coaching advice, much to the delight of the Asian Cricket Council, which can spot a few commercial advantages in getting 1.3 billion new fans.

Curiously, cricket does have some obscure links with the People's Republic. Most of us have heard of the 'Chinese Cut', an unintentional shot whereby the ball hits the inside edge of the bat, passing between batsman and wicket and away to fine leg. There is also the 'Chinaman', a term applied to a delivery from a left-arm wrist-spinner released from the back of the hand; instead of turning away from a right-handed batsman – the slow leftie's standard fare – it breaks the opposite way.

The origins of this term are debatable, but according to former Australian captain Richie Benaud it dates from 1933, when the English batsman Walter Robbins was stumped during a Manchester Test against the Windies. The bowler was Ellis 'Puss' Achong, a West Indian slow left-arm spinner of Chinese parentage, and as Robbins headed for the pavilion he muttered to the umpire, 'Fancy that. Done by a bloody Chinaman.'

— CAUGHT OUT —

To take ten wickets in a Test match is a rare and precious thing for bowlers – especially a New Zealand bowler who has just been knighted and who is in the middle of ruthlessly annihilating the cream of Australian batting. So it was for Sir Richard Hadlee at Brisbane during the 1985/6 series. Having ripped through the first eight Aussie wickets, he found himself beneath a skier from tail-ender Geoff Lawson, a batsman unlikely to resist Hadlee on any day, never mind an 'eight-for' day. Sir Richard did his duty, kissed goodbye to his Great Opportunity and pocketed the catch to give Vaughan Brown his first wicket of the day. Hadlee finished on an agonising 9–52. He never got so close again.

— CLASS OF '53 —

Picking a fantasy side of all-time England greats occupies many a wet afternoon at county grounds around the country. Cricket supporters never agree about this sort of thing, but most would surely accept the XI selected in 2004 by a *Wisden* international panel of experts as a good effort. Asked to pick a side for 'attractive, attacking cricket', they came up with the following:

Len Hutton
Graham Gooch
Peter May
Denis Compton
Ken Barrington
Ian Botham
Alan Knott
Jim Laker
Fred Trueman
Alec Bedser
Derek Underwood

This leads on to the next selection, namely the greatest England team ever to *actually* take the field together. If you accept the selection above, then the answer's fairly easy. Len Hutton's side that beat Australia at The Oval in 1953, so regaining the Ashes, also included May, Compton, Laker, Trueman and Bedser. Players and pundits might warn about the risks of comparing players from different eras, but can you honestly say that any of these six would fail to win a place in Michael Vaughan's (almost) all-conquering 2004 team? Thought not.

Incidentally, that England side of the 1950s also knew a thing or two about winning streaks. They won six straight Tests in 1957, six in 1958 and eight straight home matches in 1959/60. Within the modern game, no England team has ever dominated world cricket in quite the same way.

— HOLLYWOOD HIT —

The biggest six ever, according to *Wisden*, was struck in 1856 and travelled 175 yards, so it should be no problem for the players of Mumbles Cricket Club, Swansea, to send one a mere 150 yards and claim a £100 prize to boot.

The club's chairman, Mark Portsmouth, says he'll pay up to the first batsman who lands a ball in the garden of Catherine Zeta Jones's Swansea home, which stands on the edge of the outfield. The only catch – assuming Catherine doesn't pouch the ball the way Michael Vaughan's mum didn't (see next page) – is that the successful batsman must go and ask for it back.

— BOWLING GRIP —

Just about every cricket book ever published mentions commentary howlers, so why should this one be any different? Listeners of BBC Radio 4's *Test Match Special* will recall the late, great Brian Johnston's helpless giggles on realising that he had questioned Ian Botham's ability to 'get his leg over' (Johnners was actually referring to Botham's attempt to avoid hitting his own wicket).

Still more unfortunate – and therefore funnier – was Brian's greeting to World Service listeners as England's top order ducked and dived a West Indian bouncer onslaught during the Oval Test in 1976. His intro has since passed into broadcasting history and is a shoe-in for points at pub-quiz nights. 'You join us with the news that England are 52–3,' announced Brian. 'The bowler's Holding, the batsman's Willey.' God bless Johnners.

— READY, FREDDIE, GO —

As if glorious natural ability isn't enough to make him a headline-snatcher, Andrew 'Freddie' Flintoff has become a character straight from Boys' Own fiction. Who can forget his coy grin as he broke his bat into a V shape (should that be V sign?) while belting a ball from Makhaya Ntini into oblivion during the 2003 Lord's Test against South Africa?

Then there was the truly bizarre 'dad drama' at Edgbaston during the 2004 second Test against the West Indies. Freddie unleashed a huge six off Jermaine Lawson that, unbelievably, landed briefly in the hands of Flintoff Snr, sitting in the top tier of the Ryder Stand. This made Freddie the only England player ever to have been dropped by his dad in a Test match, a record Colin Flintoff – himself a Lancashire League player – will not be allowed to forget.

'He's got dreadful hands, has my dad,' a gleeful Freddie told reporters afterwards. 'He plays at the weekends and he always comes home and tells me what a great catch he's taken. But I think he has proved to everyone today that he's terrible. I thought he was going to fall over the balcony at one stage. He got all excited and put it down.'

Not quite true, according to Colin Flintoff's version of events. He reckons he merely deflected the cherry to the England skipper's mother. 'When you're sitting in the top deck of the stand, you normally think you're safe,' he said. 'But Andrew is such a clean striker of the ball that you can't take your eyes off it for a second. I saw it coming all the way, and I should have caught it, but in the end I parried the ball straight into Michael Vaughan's mum's lap.' She also dropped it, apparently.

— HEADY FREDDIE —

As we're on the subject, it should be said that Flintoff offers much more to his captain than mere manna for the tabloids. Not for nothing was he named ICC one-day player of the year in September 2004, posting an average of 51 runs and 12 wickets (at 20.5) in his 12 qualifying matches. Perhaps he can't yet be compared with Ian Botham, but when he received the ICC accolade, 26-year-old Freddie had scored one more six in international games (69 in ODIs, 43 in Tests) than Beefy recorded in his entire 16-year career. Whatever the arguments, the highlights of Freddie's Year make delicious reading for England supporters:

- **September 2003:** His 95 in 104 balls secures him Man of the Series Award against South Africa.

- **November 2003:** Flintoff scoops three out of three man-of-the-match awards in the one-day series against Pakistan.

- **April 2004:** Named *Wisden* Cricketer of the Year. Tears into the West Indies with 5–58.

- **July 2004:** Notches his first one-day hundred against New Zealand. Scores a jaw-dropping second against the West Indies two days later.

- **September 2004:** Signs off with a glorious 99 in 93 balls during the second one-day international against India.

Flintoff's 2003/4 Test record:

Opponents	Tests	Runs	Sixes	Wkts
S Africa	5	423	14	10
Sri Lanka	3	143	5	9
W Indies	4	200	1	11
N Zealand	3	216	3	10
W Indies	4	387	13	14
Totals	19	1369	36	54

Flintoff's One Day Internationals record (year to the end of August 2004):

Games	Runs	Sixes	Wkts
14	684	31	14

Just in case there was any doubt about Flintoff's award, he took the opportunity to smash an imperious 104 off 91 balls – his third one-day century – during England's Champions' Trophy match against Sri Lanka in September 2004.

— DOING A DELIA —

Few things in life are certain, as they say in the life-insurance ads, but in English cricket, noble traditions die hard. Village clubs can always be sure of rain, dodgy umpiring decisions and teas representing ludicrously good value for money. If the tea is produced by cookery goddess Delia Smith – as was the case at Battisford and District Cricket Club near Stowmarket, Suffolk, in the '70s and '80s – then so much the better. Scoff that upside-down cake and die happy, we say!

But, horror of horrors, it seems Delia's delights were not all they seemed. In a speech at the opening of Battisford's new pavilion in May 2004, she told how she volunteered for the tea rota during the playing days of her husband, Michael Wynn-Jones. 'I would make the teas every now and then,' she said, 'but when I was really busy I would get some sandwiches from Marks & Spencer.'

Now, that's saying nothing against M&S sarnies, which are fine examples of the genre. But talk about shattered icons! Delia's confession can be likened to Fred Trueman admitting he secretly trained as a lifestyle counsellor and Geoffrey Boycott insisting that good technique is over-rated. How *could* you, Delia?

— TV PITCH —

What would you call a massive audience for a UK TV sports event? Surely it's hard to touch England versus Germany in the Euro 2000 soccer tournament, for which the combined BBC1 and ITV audience was 17.9 million people. Yet alongside the cricket-mania of India and Pakistan, this barely troubles the scorers.

Put simply, the audience for ESPN Star (Sky TV's Asian wing) as Sachin Tendulkar strode out to bat against Pakistan in the 2004 Test series was equivalent to the combined population of Europe, ie 260 million. And that was just in India, a country of 1 billion cricket-obsessed people, most of whom don't even own a TV. Effectively, when you talk about 'sport' in India, what you mean is 'cricket'.

Understandable, then, that ESPN Star threw a wobbly on discovering in September 2004 that the Board of Control for Cricket in India had awarded four years' worth of home broadcasting rights to Zee Telefilms, the country's biggest media company. Zee outbid Star's initial $230 million (£125 million) offer by $30 million (£16 million), then – when Star hit back with $305 million (£166 million) – upped the ante still further to $308 million (£168 million). For this it will get 144 days' worth of international matches – a mouth-watering prospect for marketing men, since 75 per cent of all sports advertising in India is spent on cricket. At the time of writing, ESPN Star has challenged the BCCI's decision in the Bombay High Court.

The England and Wales Cricket Board's current contract with Sky Sports and Channel 4 (extended to the end of 2005) is worth almost £150 million, which seems, on the face of it, pretty respectable. But just consider the sponsorship spin-offs. The ECB currently allows advertising only on ground hoardings, players' and umpires' kits, TV replay screens, the boundary 'rope' (now triangular) and the stumps.

In contrast, Indian companies are bidding to sponsor anything in camera range – the ball, the bowler's run-up markers, the 30-yard field-restriction discs, the bowling speed guns, 'happy footage' of batsmen celebrating half or full centuries, TV replays (three lots, three different sponsors) and graphic versions of the scorecard. Lord knows what a dressing-room shot of Tendulkar's branded underpants would be worth.

I mention Sachin's 'shreddie potential' only because (a) he is something of a Bollywood dreamboat and (b) Indian women have a tradition of bawdy public behaviour towards Test cricketers. According to former England captain Ted Dexter, heavy flirting from the stands was a regular feature of tours to India. 'The ladies are normally segregated into a stand of their own,' he wrote in *Ted Dexter's Cricket Book* (Arthur Barker, 1963), 'and of course we always tried to send the best-looking among us to field nearest them on the boundary. Being a captain, I could never get that far afield, and I always wonder what some of those young ladies said to make the boys blush so often!'

— BATTING SHOTS —

The pull shot   **The square cut**

The back defensive   **The forward defensive**

The front-foot drive

THE PULL SHOT
HOW TO PLAY IT

- Relaxed stance, weight evenly balanced, high backswing.
- Back foot moves slightly back and across stumps. Front foot moves outside leg stump, opening shoulders.
- Head inclined forward as bat swings from above head, striking at full arm extension, finishing low.
- Body weight transfers with shot from back to bent front leg.

Sachin Tendulkar (India) – great speed and balance.
Graham Thorpe (England) – good, early positioning.

THE SQUARE CUT
HOW TO PLAY IT

- Relaxed stance, weight evenly balanced, high backswing.
- Back foot moves back and to off side (for right-hand batsmen) towards line of incoming ball. Facing shoulder turns to off side.
- Bat swings from above head with full arm extension, striking ball at waist height.
- Follow through high on other side of head.

WORTH COPYING

Andrew Strauss (England) – model footwork and timing.
Michael Clarke (Australia) – textbook 'high-to-low' follow-through.

THE BACK DEFENSIVE
HOW TO PLAY IT

- Relaxed stance, weight evenly balanced, high backswing.
- Back foot moves backwards, as close to stumps as practicable, just inside line of ball. Feet remain parallel.
- Upper body stays side-on with head still and slightly forward.
- Contact beneath eyes. Hands high, bottom hand 'soft', or relaxed. Bat vertical showing full face.

WORTH COPYING

Michael Vaughan (England) – straight bat, soft hands, perfect position.
Mark Richardson (New Zealand) – head motionless, hands high, watchful.

THE FORWARD DEFENSIVE
HOW TO PLAY IT

- Relaxed stance, weight evenly balanced, high backswing.
- Front knee bends into easy stride forward. Takes body weight as head and facing shoulder lead downswing into line of the ball.
- Contact beneath eyes, bat vertical showing full face. Back heel slightly raised to tilt upper body forward into balanced position.
- Hands high, bottom hand 'soft', or relaxed.

WORTH COPYING

Graeme Smith (South Africa) – compact, unfussy movement.
Inzamam-ul-Haq (Pakistan) – adaptability; can switch from defensive block to attacking drive mid-shot.

THE FRONT FOOT DRIVE
HOW TO PLAY IT
- Relaxed stance, weight evenly balanced, high backswing.
- Front knee bends into easy stride forward. Takes body weight as head and facing shoulder lead into line of the ball.
- Head stays still, bat accelerates through line, contact made beneath eyes.
- Bat and hands finish high.

WORTH COPYING
Mathew Hayden (Australia) – stylistically brilliant.
Michael Vaughan (England) – superb body and hands position.

— SEEING RED —

It's rare in any sport for a captain to send off one of his own players, but Derbyshire skipper Brian Bolus managed to do it in 1973, during a match against Yorkshire. Infuriated that quick bowler Alan Ward was refusing to bowl, Bolus told him, 'Right, if that's your attitude, you can get off the field and send out the 12th man. You're no use to me.'

A predictable media bunfight followed. This was, after all, only the third time in cricket history that a player had been red-carded by his captain, and among TV pundits trooping before the cameras was one FS Trueman. 'T'be a great fast bowler you 'ave to 'ave a big 'eart and a big arse,' opined Fred. 'Wardy's never 'ad neither.' The interview didn't last very long.

— LOB CULTURE —

Quick bowling is all very well but there's more than one way to flay a moggy. Step forward Sir Dawnay Lemon, former Chief Constable of the East Riding, Hampshire and Kent police forces, who was among the first-class game's last artful exponents of the underarm lob.

There's nothing in the Laws of Cricket to say you can't bowl underarm, although etiquette dictates that a batsman should get some advance warning. From the dawn of the modern game in the mid-18th century, through to the end of the 19th century, this bowling style was actually very common. Nowadays underarm deliveries are usually deployed to register contempt for slow play, although there was the notorious case of 'Trevor's Trundler' at the Melbourne Cricket Ground on 1 February 1981.

New Zealand had an outside chance of tying this game so Aussie skipper Greg Chappell instructed his older brother, Trevor, to deliver the last ball underarm to Brian McKechnie. Trevor, who had earlier trapped Richard Hadlee leg-before and bowled wicket-keeper Ian Smith, duly obliged. The tactic worked and both brothers were ruthlessly monstered by the world's press as unsporting cads! Cricket, let's remember, is the only game in the world in which a player gets pilloried for obeying the rules.

Sir Dawnay, who died aged 92 in August 2004, must have been appalled at Chappell's treatment, although his canny lobs were very different in nature. Lemon liked to send the ball sailing high in the air, baffling batsmen with its flight, while simultaneously imparting vicious spin.

Much more Trevor-like was the action of Lord Hazlerigg, who turned out regularly for the MCC during the 1930s. On a good day his low skidders were said to be unplayable.

— NAME CHECK —

His first name is Harold, and he's known universally as 'Dickie', but in fact former Test umpire Harold Bird has always been known to his family as Dennis, his middle name. His mum, dad and sister apparently 'never bothered with the Harold bit'.

— OH MAN —

Commentators come and go, but the memory of broadcasting genius John Arlott lingers on. Perhaps his greatest one-liner – and there were many – came when England skipper George Mann took on South Africa's left-arm spinner Tufty Mann in the MCC's 1948/9 tour and smashed him for six. 'That,' said Arlott, 'was a perfect example of Mann's inhumanity to Mann.'

Incidentally, George is one of only two sets of fathers and sons to have captained their countries at Test cricket. His dad, Frank (who also skippered a South African tour in 1922–3), was a fearsome striker of the ball who once hit a six at Lord's that landed in St John's Wood Road. The other father-and-son combo are India's Pataudis. The Nawab of Pataudi, Jnr (to give him his aristocratic title), was only 21 when he became captain of India. He was also the only Test player who arrived for games in his own private jet.

— BATTING DEPTH —

You'll often hear commentators describe a side that 'bats a long way down' (meaning that the bowlers can wield the willow, too), but these things are all relative. Few teams have batted quite so far down as the 'Farmers', who took on Mr Tankerville Chamberlayne's XI in an exhibition match at his country seat at Yatton, near Bristol, in October 1887. This is because the Farmers had 45 in their team.

Yatton, though, had quality in the shape of the well-known amateur cricketer OG Radcliffe, who claimed 11 victims in the match. Just four wickets fell to (early) catches, according to a scorecard published in *Cricket* magazine of 27 October 1887. Perhaps the scorers quickly decided that such detail was rather too trivial.

However, 'rather too trivial' is a concept unrecognisable to us here, so fasten up your anorak and wallow away in the stuff they *did* manage to record between pints of foaming ale. We have to assume that the match was drawn, although that isn't absolutely clear from the card.

FARMERS		YATTON	
B Marshall b Chamberlayne	20	C Knowles b Luff	7
B Burgess run out	1	AE Clapp ret	20
C Hawkins b Radcliffe	0	EW Blew c Gill b Luff	18
J Pavey run out	0	H Gage ret	23
J Hill b Radcliffe	0	T Chamberlayne b Luff	0
SB Griffin run out	2	WA Winter run out	3
J Edgell c Clapp b Radcliffe	2	WH Shiner not out	1
A Williams c & b Radcliffe	4	Extras	3
T Price c & b Radcliffe	0		
A Osmond b Chamberlayne	0	Total	75–6
T Champion b Radcliffe	0		
W Cavill b Chamberlayne	0		
H Wail b Gage	0		
W Marsh b Radcliffe	0		
R Wilcox b Gage	0		
MH Thatcher b Winter	0		
W Gill b Clapp	0		
J Wallis b Winter	0		
W Hennessy b Gage	0		
R Harding b Blew	0		
FW Wills run out	1		
C Burgess b Clapp	0		
J Gage b Clapp	10		
G Hardwick b Blew	3		
W Luff b Blew	0		
G Badman b Blew	0		
SM Harding run out	2		
A Batt b Radcliffe	4		
T Pearce b Shiner	12		
C Griffin b Radcliffe	0		
H Morgan b Shiner	0		
T Nicholls b Radcliffe	2		
A Hardwick b Shiner	0		
A Williams b Radcliffe	1		
C Sayer b Atherton	2		
J Bisder b Shiner	2		
C Young b Atherton	0		
H Macey b Atherton	0		
W Petheran b Gage	4		
JH Fowler b Gage	0		
S Hurley not out	1		
Extras	8		
Total (all out)	92		

— HURRAH FOR MANNERS —

Etiquette is synonymous with cricket, apparently, so to save your blushes, here's the definitive Aggers' Guide. Village cricketers have different standards to professionals, so we've helpfully come up with a number of scenarios to guide you through the maze.

INCOMING BATSMEN

VILLAGERS: Clap politely and make inconsequential remarks about the weather.

PROS: Eyeball menacingly and question batsman's parentage. (Note: In women's game, slip fielders should loudly complain that they 'can't see the ball past her arse'.)

CAUGHT BEHIND OFF FAINT TICKLE

VILLAGERS: Don't look back. Adopt pained expression before meaningfully placing bat under arm and removing gloves. Walk purposefully to pavilion with head held high and rueful smile. Throw bat at dressing-room wall.

PROS: Look back guiltily to see if catch is taken. Immediately remember this is tell-tale sign, so lean on bat and smile in patronising way suggesting slips are rotten cheats. If given out, stand in stunned amazement for several seconds (but not too long to get fined). Drag self off pitch looking back constantly at big-screen replay. Shake head frequently. Scowl. Roll eyes to sky. Throw bat at dressing-room wall.

UMPIRE TURNS DOWN BOWLER'S APPEAL

VILLAGERS: Accept umpire's decision. If *really* frustrated, try shouting, "Ow's that one, then?' when next appealing, implying that first refusal was travesty of justice.

PROS: Incline head and purse lips, taking sharp intake of breath when receiving sweater from umpire at end of over. Appeal more loudly next time. Wave arms more.

SHINING AND 'IMPROVING' THE BALL

VILLAGERS: Don't bother.

PROS: Rub hard on all parts of body, ensuring that red polish gives look of film extra from *Saving Private Ryan*. Pick seam and scratch non-shiny side with stone to improve swing. Rub oily suncream from face onto shiny side of ball.

NB: Theoretically, polishing, drying or removing mud from the ball is all that's allowed.

DANGEROUS BOWLING

VILLAGERS: Always say sorry to batsman after bowling beamer (head-high full toss). Unintentionally bowl another. Repeat as necessary.

PROS: Never say sorry to batsman after bowling a bouncer. Intentionally bowl another. Repeat until warned by umpire. Then adopt facial expression suitable for witnessing second coming of Christ.

Among other antics considered bad form – but rarely seen – are time wasting and stealing runs (ie batsmen nicking a single as the bowler runs up). There is a five-run penalty for both offences. Players can also be penalised for damaging the pitch (ie roughing up the 'protected' ground in front of either wicket). This area is an imaginary rectangle extending one foot across either side of middle stump and five feet down the pitch.

— TAKING COVER —

Cricket is such a rich and varied game that almost nothing surprises you. However, one groundsman came within minutes of cancelling a cup game at South Shields after seagulls first laid an egg on his square – then kept attacking him as he tried to move it.

The bizarre Hitchcock-esque drama ended in an hour-long stand-off as 50-year-old Robin Wightman dodged their persistent attempts to 'dive-bomb' him. Eventually he managed to sneak up, grab the egg and remove the birds' makeshift nest. 'A number of times they swooped and missed my head by inches,' said Mr Wightman. 'They were frightening and could have put the match in jeopardy.'

— BARRACKING SISTERS —

One of Australia's great wartime heroes, Lieutenant General Sir Tom Daly, CB, KBE, CBE, DSO, OBE was a fanatical cricket fan who took pride in teaching his three daughters the intricacies of the game. A crucial part of this education included guidance on barracking the opposition. One can only imagine the scene at the boundary as the Daly girls let fly at some hapless Long Leg strolling harmlessly by.

Lt Gen Daly, who saw off the Japanese in the last big Allied operation of the Second World War – the seaborne assault on Borneo – was once asked what he'd have done if he'd had a son. 'Strapped his right arm to his side,' he replied. 'Australia desperately needs a left-arm bowler.'

— CAPTAIN'S LOG —

Does acquiring the England captaincy affect a player's performance? Definitely, according to Mike Atherton, who reckons the first three years of his spell improved his performance while the last 18 months dragged him down. 'I couldn't set aside as much time for practice,' he wrote in his *Sunday Telegraph* column. 'I became embroiled in the politics of selection and arguments about the system; I felt knackered all the time; defeats affected my confidence; adverse press wasn't helpful – all with the result that I couldn't walk to the crease with a clear head – an essential requirement for scoring runs.'

In Vaughan's case, the cold statistics support Athers' theory. The figures below cover his career up until July 2004 .

TESTS PRE-CAPTAINCY

Opponents	Matches	Runs	H/score	Average	100s	50s
Australia	5	633	183	63	3	0
India	6	721	197	90.12	3	2
N Zealand	3	131	36	21.83	0	0
Pakistan	2	166	120	55.33	1	0
South Africa	5	382	156	42.44	1	1
Sri Lanka	4	319	115	53.16	1	1
West Indies	4	169	76	28.16	0	1
Zimbabwe	2	28	20	14.00	0	0
Totals	31	2549	197	50.98	9	5

TESTS AS CAPTAIN

Opponents	Matches	Runs	H/score	Average	100s	50s
Bangladesh	2	208	81	69.33	0	2
N Zealand	2	84	61	28.00	0	1
South Africa	4	140	33	17.50	0	0
Sri Lanka	3	221	105	36.83	1	1
West Indies	4	245	140	35.00	1	0
Totals	15	898	140	33.25	2	4

Of course, no one in his right mind would suggest that Vaughan is anything other than class. Yet the captaincy curse can't be ignored, especially as it also applies to one-day cricket. Here, at least, Vaughan is in esteemed company. His average of around 23 (July 2004) is uncannily close to the ODI records of his predecessors – Alec Stewart (23.10 in 41 matches), David Gower (25.04 in 24), Graham Gooch (29.95 in 50) and Nasser Hussain (31.33 in 56). For the record, England's best ODI batting average for a skipper is 33.95 in 43 games – held by Atherton.

— TRENDY LEFTIES —

The received wisdom among Test selectors is that left-handed batsman have an in-built advantage. Now scientists at the University of New South Wales in Sydney have proved it. Sort of.

According to the UNSW team, only a quarter of the 177 players who batted in the 2003 World Cup were left-handers, yet they together occupied almost half the available top three places in batting orders. There was also a correlation between the most successful teams and the number of left-handers they contained; competition winners Australia, for instance, sent out four in its top six.

The reason for this is not because lefties are better. That would be much too simple. It's all down to something called 'negative frequency dependent effect', which, broadly speaking, means that bowlers are less used to aiming at left-handers, and so their performance suffers as a result. Wonderful thing, education.

— WARNE'S WORLD —

How to describe Shane Warne? Bowling magician? Iron-willed competitor? Flawed genius? Well built? Answer: All of the above. At the time of writing, Warne is locked in a personal duel with that other Sultan of Spin, Sri Lanka's Muttiah 'Murali' Muralitharan. Each wants to be the greatest Test wicket-taker of all time. Each is edging towards the 550 mark. And yet each, for different reasons, has his demons to conquer.

More of Murali later but here's a quick primer on Warney's ups and downs.

1969   UP: Shane is born in Melbourne on 13 September. Not technically an 'up' from a cricketing point of view, but only saddo readers should formally complain.

1990   DOWN: Kicked out of the Australian Cricket Academy for disciplinary reasons.

1992   UP: Makes Test debut against India.

1992   DOWN: In two of the Tests he notches a combined return of 1 for 228.

1993   UP: Bags 7 for 52 against the Windies in his home town. Takes 17 wickets in three Tests against the Kiwis. Bowls Mike Gatting first ball at Old Trafford – Shane's first Test appearance in England.

1994   DOWN: Australia's tour manager in Pakistan, Colin Egar, hears allegations of Warne's involvement in a match-fixing scandal, a supposed bribe from Salim Malik to throw the Karachi Test. ICC is informed.

1994   UP: Leading wicket-taker in all three series. Finishes with a delicious hat-trick in Melbourne against the Poms.

1995   DOWN: Is fined, together with Mark Waugh, after admitting taking money from bookmaker in return for tips on 'pitch and weather conditions'.

1996   DOWN: Major injury problems. Needs treatment for dodgy shoulder and surgery to main spinning finger. Misses short tour to India.

1997   UP: Helps Australia retain the Ashes in England with a contribution of 24 wickets and 188 runs.

1999   UP: Wins Man of the Match Award in the Aussies' World Cup victory over Pakistan.

2000   UP: Becomes Australia's greatest Test wicket-taker, overtaking Dennis Lillee's 355 during a tour of New Zealand.

2000   UP: *Wisden* names Warne among five Cricketers of the Century.

2001   UP: Helps Australia retain the Ashes 4–1, claiming 31 wickets and carding 11–229 in the final Test at the Oval.

2002   UP: Takes 27 wickets against Pakistan, beating Lillee and Richie Benaud's joint Australian record for most wickets by an Australian in a three-Test series.

2003   DOWN: Banned for 12 months by the Australian Cricket Board for taking the banned substances hydrochlorothiazide and amiloride. Angrily denies the allegation, claiming his mum, Brigitte, just gave him a diuretic.

— BEEFY BUFF —

Neither Bob Willis nor Ian Botham has ever cultivated a culture-vulture image, although it seems they do like a nice drop of wine. The heroes of the 1981 Ashes have teamed up with Australian wine-maker Geoff Merrill to launch a label called BMW (that's Botham, Merrill, Willis, in case you were wondering), conceived after Merrill overhead Big Bob describe Australian beer as 'weasel piss'.

The BMW brand was launched in 2003 with an 'herbaceous' cabernet sauvignon – *cab sav* to our Australian readership – and a 'lightly oaked melon and citrus chardonnay'. Willis is keen to stress that this isn't just another celebrity wine endorsement. 'Geoff didn't just point to a spare vat of wine and say, "Stick your names on that, lads,"' he says. 'These are the wines we like to drink.'

Heaven forbid that any England cricketer, past or present, would stoop to gain filthy lucre from endorsing a product he didn't really enjoy. Botham, though, admits he's not a great one for the lightly oaked stuff. 'To be honest, I like the whites big, oaky and strong,' he says. 'But Bob falls over if it's stronger than 12 per cent.'

— EDDIE'S LAW —

The gifted South African all-rounder Eddie Barlow had a reputation for playing hard but fair. To him, 'walking' before you'd been given out was a ludicrous notion, as he once explained to the doyen of English Test umpires, Dickie Bird.

In his excellent memoirs *White Cap And Bails*, Bird recounts the conversation thus: "'I've got away with a lot, Dickie. I've been given not-out when I should have been out. But, then again, I've been given out when I knew I wasn't. It's swings and roundabouts. Either way, I never complain. I go back to the dressing room, take off my pads and gloves, and say nothing. I accept decisions, good or bad, because they even themselves out in the long run.

'"But I *never* walk."'

— COUNTY SET —

Backroom politics is a feature of most sports, but the edginess between the English counties and the game's governing body, the England and Wales Cricket Board, is the stuff of legend. Machiaevelli is an also-ran alongside certain – though not all – members of cricket's blazer brigade, and recently in-house tension between the two camps has turned into open internecine warfare. So it was when ECB chief executive Tim Lamb, his communications director John Read and Mark Sibley, the Board's commercial director, all quit in 2004. They'd apparently had enough of the tail (the counties) wagging the dog (the England team).

In an interview with the *Sunday Telegraph*, Read led the attack on county chairmen. He pointed out that, since 90 per cent of the ECB's annual £60 million income was generated by the England Test team – the 'powerhouse' – that team's administrators should be given enhanced powers to shape overall strategy. He cited the successful launch of Twenty20 cricket, which replaced the old Benson and Hedges Cup, and the way it was almost strangled at birth by county chairmen. 'Were it not for the decisive, courageous and crucial behind-the-scenes intervention of Lord MacLaurin, then chairman of the ECB...then the vote may well have been lost,' said Read. 'As it was, six county chairmen voted against progress. In an era of fast consumption,

Twenty20 has been a huge success, and the ECB and counties who supported its introduction deserve praise.'

Of course, the county clubs argue that they find the Test stars in the first place, coach them, tend their injuries, find them sponsors, pay their wages and generally help them blossom. Counties see themselves as the crucial link between school, club and supporter level and a successful England side. Read is unconvinced.

'The hidden-hand influence often exerted by county members via pressure on their county chairmen, which is out of all proportion to their importance to the wider game, must be blunted,' he said. 'County members typically pay £2 per day to watch first-class cricket. It seems absurd that they should exert any influence over their own county, let alone the future of English cricket.' Hmmm.

— ICC TEST CHAMPIONSHIP TABLE —

	Matches	Points	Rating
Australia	45	5933	132
England	49	5396	110
India	39	4209	108
Sri Lanka	35	3613	103
Pakistan	31	3145	101
South Africa	43	4247	99
New Zealand	31	2891	93
West Indies	37	2717	73
Zimbabwe	25	1045	42
Bangladesh	35	220	6

— CAP THAT —

Record books are stuffed with cricketers who've turned out just the once for their country. Like one-hit wonders of the pop world, they are destined to be consigned to the historical dustbin of trivia, to be retrieved only by close family members, statto fiends and authors needing to fill space fast.

Test careers are made and broken on matters of luck as much as anything, so bear in mind that the following's appearance in our Fantasy Single-Cappers' XI doesn't mean *ipso facto* that they were all bad players, just that they were never destined for greatness.

OK, some were plain useless.

FRED GRACE

With that surname, he should have gone far, but WG's lesser-known brother is best remembered for the catch he took in his only Test (against the visiting Aussies in 1880) to get rid of the Herculean figure of George Bonnor. It's said that, after spanking the ball skywards, Bonnor and his partner crossed twice before Fred pouched it – which just proves either that (a) cricket folklore is a load of baloney or (b) the batsmen had each dropped a tab of amphetamine while padding up. Anyway, Fred didn't trouble the scorers in either of his innings, and it was left to his skipper, old WG himself, to secure a win by hitting England's first century in Test cricket.

FRANCIS ALEXANDER MACKINNON, THE 35TH MACKINNON OF MACKINNON

His period in Test cricket was not dissimilar to the time taken to pronounce his name (he scored 0 and 5 at Melbourne in 1879). However, he made his mark on the game by being part of Freddie Spofforth's hat-trick – the first ever in Test cricket. MacKinnon etc's selection really should baffle cricket historians, given that his first-class average was a pitiful 16.42 in ten years. Then again, you don't get a moniker like that living in the East End.

GEORGE EMMETT

The selectors must have had it in for the diminutive Emmett. He was picked for the 1948 third Test against Australia instead of some bloke called Len Hutton, who was considered to have performed poorly in the two previous games, scoring 3, 74, 20 and 13. You might say that an average of 27.5 against Lindwall and Miller isn't *that* poor, and that only a bunch of airheads would drop one of England's greatest ever batsmen for the first time since his debut in 1937. Still, drop him they did. The inexperienced Emmett flopped with 10 and 0. So it was back to Plan A for the fourth Test, in which Hutton made 81 and 57.

THE HON CHARLES COVENTRY

Coventry had never played first-class cricket before when he was selected to bat at number 10 for England in the 1888–9 series against South Africa. It certainly showed. He made 12 and 1 not out. Still, he must have seemed like a nice chap from a good background. Otherwise, why pick him?

JOSEPH McMASTER

Oh dear. McMaster was one of the Hon Charles's teammates. He wasn't a bowler and batted at number 11, scoring a duck in his only first-class innings. He and Charles were obviously the result of a good lunch washed down with a passable claret at someone's dining club. The pair's lack of skill is even more embarrassing given that South Africa were so weak (it was their first Test series) that their combined total in the second game was 90.

JACK MACBRYAN

MacBryan had the hard-luck story to rival them all. Picked for Test honours in 1924, he never got the chance to bat or bowl and his one game as an England player was washed out by rain. His contribution was (probably) the shortest ever in a Test match: three hours.

— CAP THAT (CONT'D) —

CHARLES PALMER

Long before he was my Leicestershire chairman, Palmer was an amateur player, chosen to be tour manager for the 1953–4 West Indies tour. The great cricket correspondent EW Swanton called his appointment 'just about the worst decision ever to come out of Lord's', which is saying something. Anyway, things went from bad to staggeringly dreadful when the team selectors actually *picked* Palmer for the Barbados Test ahead of the pro Ken Suttle (who had just made 96 and 62 on the same ground). Palmer scored 22 and 0 and returned bowling figures of 0–15. Suttle went on to score 29,375 runs for Sussex. He must have wondered what you had to do to get an England cap. Let's not go there.

LELAND HONE

Hone was a last-minute selection as wicket-keeper in a 1878/9 Ashes match at Melbourne. He clung on to a couple of catches, but his 7 and 6 with the bat ensured he never got a second cap.

TONY PIGOTT

Another victim of Lady Luck, Pigott was playing club cricket in New Zealand when he was summoned to join a touring MCC party that had lost Neil Foster and Graham Dilley to injury ahead of the Second Test. Pigott, who was due to get married on the fourth day of the match, was criticised for being tired and nervous. He was certainly tired, having played a first-class game the previous day, yet his 2 for 75 off 17 was hardly the worst return imaginable – especially given that Ian Botham shipped 88 runs off the same number of overs. Pigott never played again and could have kept his wedding date. New Zealand wrapped things up by an innings inside three days to help secure their first series win over England.

CECIL COOK

Slow left-armer Cook was given a near-impossible task when he was thrown into the side on a peach of a wicket at Trent Bridge during the 1947 series against South Africa. His figures were 0–87 and 0–40 and he contributed 0 and 4 with the bat.

KEN PALMER

Better known for his later career as a Test umpire, Palmer was another willing journeyman called up to solve an injury crisis, this time during England's 1964/5 tour of South Africa. Plucked from the coaching school in Johannesburg, where he was wintering, Palmer's only Test wicket cost him 189 runs.

— AUSSIE RULES —

When England won a victory in the fourth test of the 2001 Ashes series – something of a consolation prize – the BBC was keen to get reaction from a senior player. A researcher was briefed to 'get someone on the phone' and a call went through to the England party at their hotel.

'Alec Stewart' duly came on the line and was immediately patched through to interviewer Gary Richardson. 'How are you, Alec? It was a good way to finish,' ventured Richardson. 'Yeah, it was tremendous,' said an Aussie voice clearly not that of England's 'keeper. 'What have England learned from the Ashes'? continued Gary, nervously. 'That Australia are a bloody good team,' said 'Alec'. The call was cut short.

— CLOSE SHAVE —

One way to improve your chance of hitting a big six is to use a bigger bat. OK up to a point, but the Laws of Cricket demand that the maximum width is 4.25 inches. When ICC match referee Clive Lloyd conducted a random check before the Zimbabwe–India match in Harare in 2002, he found that 'several players from both sides' were playing with illegally broad bats.

The manufacturer of the Indians' kit telephoned skipper Sourav Ganguly to explain that facing tape – used by players to protect bat surfaces – was responsible. 'If [Ganguly] removes that tape, the bat will be exactly the normal size,' said Jatin Sareen, MD of Sareen Sports. The ICC said that all the dodgy ones were later 'adjusted to within legal parameters'. It is understood that several cricketers had a hard sandpapering session before their innings.

— BIG CHERRY —

Unlikely though it sounds, New York City is leading America's cricket revolution. With more than 100 clubs and 5,000 participants in the Big Apple alone, the city's 64 pitches are in hot demand among team skippers. It's a kind of turf war without guns. At least, no one's mentioned guns yet.

According to the US Cricket Association, 15,000 players are registered – from New Jersey to Chicago and California – while the nation's first dedicated stadium has just been built in Fort Lauderdale, Florida. In the New York League, leading Caribbean players can earn up to $10,000 (£5,450) for a three-week guest stint, and former stars such as Sir Viv Richards are treated like gods on their occasional visits to Van Cortland Park, in the Bronx, for exhibition matches.

A top trivia point to mention here is that the first-ever international cricket match between representative teams was not – as is sometimes claimed – the inaugural Australia vs England game at the Melbourne Cricket Ground in March 1877. International cricket actually began on 24 September 1844, when the USA lined up against Canada on a field used by the St George's Club near Bloomingdale Road, New York City. The first ball, incidentally, was an underarm lob delivered by America's top bowler, H Groom. It was received by Canada's opening batsman, D Winckworth.

So why, given that New York is the birthplace of international cricket, has it taken so long for the game to get going? Part of the reason is Uncle Sam's obsession with baseball, basketball and American football, all of which have long been embraced by high schools and college jocks. Against this culture, cricket is viewed as a slightly eccentric, puzzling pastime (not wrong there, then) executed by expatriate Brits working on Wall Street, the foreign press corps and a few unknown Limey actors.

For decades it seemed that the only natives clued in to the rules were the upper classes of New England and Pennsylvania (the latter's Philadelphia Cricket Club is about as close to Lord's as you're ever likely to get in America). However, the arrival of immigrants from Pakistan, India and (especially) the Caribbean has changed everything.

The spiritual home of US cricket is now Singh's Sporting Goods, in New York's tough Queens district, where the world's finest bats are drooled over on a daily basis. The owner, Dupaul Singh, says he was keen to compare his wares with those of the prestigious London sports retailer Lillywhites. During a cricket tour to the UK in 1995, he fulfilled a 'boyhood dream' and ventured inside the store for a nose around. 'Then I saw that I stock more stuff than they do,' he told the *Daily Telegraph*. 'I'm selling 1,000 bats a year.'

In the same article, USCA chairman Paul DaSilva – who emigrated from Guyana in the 1980s – claims cricket has taken off because it's viewed as a family pastime ideal for city parks. 'We are already a bigger cricket market than in the UK,' he said. 'Cricket may never be the game of white guys in the Midwest, but in New York and Florida and California it's going mainstream.'

Readers wanting to visit the spot where that first USA vs Canada game was played should walk along East 31st Street to the New York University Medical Center. (It's possible that the actual field may not be there anymore.)

— BOOTING UP —

If you were starting from scratch, you'd think long and hard about cricket's laws on bowling actions. It's not just the ever-present chucking controversy; fast bowlers place their bodies under enormous strain during run-up and delivery, particularly the bone-mashing impact of the front foot. Andy Caddick, Darren Gough and Devon Malcolm have all been martyrs to this kind of injury.

Now, however, Iain Sabberton, a sports graduate of Northumbria University, has developed a boot on which studs are attached to a flexible plate. Smaller, secondary studs are then placed either side, with the result that the impact on foot joints is reduced. Patents are in place and the new-style boots should be in shops any day now.

— WHATZAT NOISE? —

The 2004 ICC Champions' Trophy was the first major tournament to use stump microphones capable of transmitting the faintest bat-on-ball nick to umpires via an earpiece. In fact, umpires were less concerned by this innovation than by a new rule requiring no-balls to be called by off-field colleagues studying TV footage. Veteran English umpire David Shepherd admitted that years of habit would compel him to raise his arm and shout 'NO BALL' – whether he was supposed to or not.

— BAT OFF! —

Ah, you can't beat British justice. However British justice can certainly beat you, as a burglar foolish enough to break into the Exeter, Devon, home of Judge Martin Meeke, QC, discovered. 'I picked up a cricket bat as I impressed upon him that he was not leaving the room,' Mr Meeke later told a jury. 'If he had tried to go, I would have used the bat, but I didn't have to.'

Readers will no doubt be wondering whether the judge intended a stylish cover drive, a pull, a late cut or – and this would have been *really* controversial – a reverse sweep. Sadly, the prosecution barrister never asked such obvious questions and seemed more concerned with the tone of the intruder's language. 'There was nothing wrong with his language,' replied Mr Meeke. 'There may have been a good deal wrong with mine.'

— DUNCAN'S WAY —

When Duncan Fletcher was appointed England coach in 1999, he inherited a grossly under-performing England side. Realising that nothing would change unless he got more time with his players, Fletcher pursued the idea of ECB central contracts with quiet zeal, seeing off the predictable protests of county chairmen, coaches and chief execs. As 2004 drew to a close, and with England's superb run of eight straight Test wins safely in the bank, that rumbling in the shires seemed somehow muffled.

Of course, any follower of international cricket knows that underestimating Fletcher is a dangerous game. Because he is a Zimbabwean, some opponents have hinted that he has never been fully exposed to the pressure-keg of top-level Test cricket – never smelled the cannon smoke of, say, an Ashes decider or India vs Pakistan showdown. Unfortunately for them, Fletcher's record confirms the opposite; he was a gifted all-rounder and captain of his country who consistently got players to punch above their weight.

His finest hour came during the 1983 World Cup at Trent Bridge, Nottingham. Fletcher led from the front to humble one of Australia's greatest World Cup sides, scoring 69 at number six against Jeff Thomson, Dennis Lillee, Geoff Lawson and Rodney Hogg. Maybe that quartet doesn't count as 'proper' pressure, although, aside from stepping into the ring with Mike Tyson at his peak, it's hard to think of another scenario in world sport that comes remotely close. Fletcher didn't do too badly with the ball that day, either; the victims in his 4-42 were Graeme Wood, Kim Hughes, David Hookes and Graham Yallop.

Fletcher is not infallible. Some criticisms of his style are valid. But pressure? He knows about pressure.

— TAME TIGERS —

There are times when sledging really isn't sensible – such as when your opponents are the Liberation Tigers of Tamileelam, otherwise known as the Tamil Tigers. A cease-fire in the long-running Sri Lankan civil war had allowed fighters from the guerrilla group to resume their national passion for cricket.

In their first friendly game they took on a hospital side in Batticaloa, an eastern provincial town, scoring 250 runs in 20 overs and dismissing the medics for just 14. Sledging the Tigers' batsmen was never a serious option, but the scorecard suggests the hospital team tried really hard not to upset them in any way – say, by trying to win.

— BARMY BONANZA —

It sounds unlikely, but England's 'Barmy Army' of travelling supporters have struck a real chord among Australians. Well, that's not strictly true; we're talking specifically here about Australians in charge of tourism.

After watching 16,000 England supporters cram into the Sydney cricket ground during the last Ashes humiliation, Australia has realised the economic benefits that come with beer-swilling, free-spending and – it must be said – generally good-humoured Pommie cricket-lovers. David Peacock, co-founder of the Barmy Army tour company, reckons each fan drinks around 12 pints and spends about £100 per day. 'We love them,' said Lois Appleby, chief executive of Tourism Victoria, which plans to use pictures of the Army in advertising campaigns. 'We are going to target sports fans increasingly.'

Australian cricketers aren't so sure. In recent years they've been subjected to some cutting satire during Test matches, mostly in the form of well-known songs that have been, er, adapted. If you've read about the downs of Shane Warne's career (see page 36–7), you'll get the drift of this first one straight away. It's sung to the tune of 'How Much Is That Doggy In The Window?' All lyrics courtesy of the Barmy Army website.

> *How much can we pay you for the weather?*
> *How much for the state of the pitch?*
> *How much for the state of the leather?*
> *Oh, fat boy we will make you rich.*

Then there's a rather ruder one to the tune of 'My Old Man's A Dustman'. 'Hickey' is, of course, Graeme Hick.

> *Shane Warne is an Aussie*
> *He wears a baggy cap*
> *He wears a Nike earing*
> *He is an Aussie twat*
> *He's got his little flipper*
> *He's got his box of tricks*
> *But when he bowls at Hickey*
> *He hits him for a six*

Naturally, the Barmy Army also prides itself on geeing up the England side through powerful lyrics sung to stirring nationalistic melodies. Think how this one, trotted out to the tune of 'Rupert The Bear', must have inspired the leadership of captain Nasser Hussain whenever the going got rough.

Nasser, Nasser Hussain
Everyone knows his name
Nasser, Nasser Hussain
Everyone knows his name
It's Nasser Hussain

AWARDS FOR ACIDIC GIBES AND GOBSMACKINGLY EXPLOSIVE RIPOSTES — (THE AGGERS) —

...FOR MALE COACHES IN TOUCH WITH THEIR FEMININE SIDE:
'If the players expect soft drinks, I will make sure there are none. They will go to a tap and get on their knees and drink water until they realise that it is an honour to play for South Africa.'
– South Africa coach Ray Jennings

...FOR MAINTAINING PERSPECTIVE
'I'll tell you what pressure is. Pressure is a Messerschmitt up your arse. Playing cricket is not.'
– Awarded posthumously to former RAF World War II Mosquito pilot and Aussie all-rounder Keith Miller

...FOR TELLING IT STRAIGHT
'Sachin Tendulkar is, in my time, the best player without doubt. Daylight second. Brian Lara third.'
– Shane Warne

...FOR CULINARY ADVENTURE ON TOUR
'Nothing against Indian food and all that, but I get sick over here. Hopefully I'm better prepared this time. I've got my protein shakes, a few tins of spaghetti, a few tins of beans. I've got some cereal. Some people don't like seafood. I just don't like curry.'
– Shane Warne

— THE AGGERS (CONT'D) —

...FOR LITERARY ANALOGY
'[Brian Lara] has also had the great misfortune to be captaining the West Indies at their lowest ebb. Captain Ahab couldn't stop this ship from sinking.'

– Michael Atherton

...FOR TWO-FINGERED RIPOSTES
'I don't need more awards. I already have the world record.'

– Muttiah Muralitharan (on being excluded from an ICC World XI)

...FOR REVERSE PSYCHOLOGY
'Mind the windows, Tino.'

– Andrew Flintoff (two balls before Tino Best got stumped off a wild swing at the 2004 Lord's Test)

...FOR UNDERSTATED SARCASM
'Gussie [Angus Fraser], you know I'm not the sort who says much in the middle.'

– Glenn McGrath

...FOR DIPLOMATIC FINESSE
'They are rubbish wickets, really.'

– Kiwi Scott Styris on the pride of England's county grounds.

...FOR RESPECT
'If you get Dravid, great. If you get Sachin, brilliant. If you get Laxman, it's either a mistake or a miracle.'

– Steve Waugh (before Australia's 2004 tourists destroyed the Indians)

...FOR COMPETITIVE INSTINCTS
'I think the important thing about this competition [ICC Champions' Trophy] is that we've never won it.'

– Matthew Hayden

...FOR MOST BAFFLING SLEDGE
'I ask them [batsmen] what movies they've seen recently.'

– Harbhajan Singh

...For Heart On Sleeve

'He keeps chucking me the ball, which is an absolute pain in the arse.'

> – *Darren Lehmann criticising his Yorkshire captain and brother-in-law Craig White.*

...For Academic Analysis

'Boy George would be considered straight at the University of Western Australia.'

> – *Aussie Test player-turned-commentator Kerry O'Keeffe on UWA's controversial assessment of Muralitharan's bowling action.*

...For Brutal Honesty

'I'm not going to write off Bangladesh. The way we're playing right now, you can't write off anybody at all.'

> – *Brian Lara*

...For Constructive Criticism

'I'm not saying the players will get any better. But they can't get any worse.'

> – *Colin Croft, former Windies paceman*

...For Technical Analysis

'Corey Collymore and Adam Sanford wouldn't bowl my mum out.'

> – *Geoffrey Boycott*

'All those queuing up for the [Indian] opening slot don't have it in them. They are all crap.'

> – *Geoffrey Boycott*

...For Fence Sitting

'Those who run cricket in this country, especially at the domestic level, are for the most part a self-serving, pusillanimous and self-important bunch of myopic dinosaurs unable to take any but the shortest-term view of everything.'

> – *Henry Blofeld*

...For Abstinence

'I don't think I've actually drunk a beer for 15 years, except for a few Guinnesses in Dublin, where it's the law.'

> – *Ian Botham*

— PETTY FOUR —

Nasser Hussain fans were outraged when in May 2004 he was docked three runs off his last shot in Test Cricket – a majestic four to win the Lord's Test against New Zealand. Hussain was on 102 not out when he stroked the ball past extra cover and over the boundary rope, yet the official scorecard left him on 103.

The reason? That four never counted. Law 21.6 states that 'as soon as a result is reached, the match is at an end. Nothing that happens thereafter will be regarded as part of the match.' You might feel there's no real need for a rule which states that a match finishes when it is finished, but that Hussain drive would prove you wrong. By the time the ball crossed the rope, Hussain had already run the single required to win and the match was over. Without rigorous application of Law 21.6 he would have retired scoring a third consecutive four to win a Test at the Home of Cricket. And that would have been terrible. Wouldn't it?

— HEAD CASES —

Some cynics think academics dream up truly off-the-wall research ideas for a bet, or at least a good laugh. Not true, of course, for the human cognitive neuroscience unit at Northumbria University, Newcastle upon Tyne, which has discovered that cricket helmets slow the brain by making batsmen's heads hot. Put another way, according to research leader Dr Nick Neave, 'In young adults, in a mild climate, some aspects of cognition are affected by wearing a non-vented protective helmet following exercise.'

Dr Neave reached this conclusion after getting 16 young colts from Durham County Cricket Club to bat against a bowling machine. Half of them wore standard helmets and later went through a computerised test for mental abilities such as reaction times, vigilance and attentiveness. Dr Neave discovered that getting hot had no effect on the cricketers' physical responses, nor on their ability to perform simple mental tasks. But when they were set more complex challenges, such as making choices, their reaction times dropped, in one case by 16 milliseconds. At Test level, this could mean the difference between a quick single and a long trudge to the pavilion. However, as Dr Neave stresses, 'Cricketers should not disregard safety. Getting run out may be preferable to brain damage.'

Of course, helmets don't always help. The Zimbabwe batsman Mark Vermeulen suffered two skull fractures by the age of 25: one incurred during a nets session against his team-mate Travis Friend, the second courtesy of Indian seamer Irfan Pathan during a 2004 triangular tournament in Australia. He'd worn a helmet on both occasions.

Vermeulen's later injury meant that his skull had to be sliced open from ear to ear and three titanium plates inserted to replace his shattered bones. Doctors have since told him that a third strike in the same spot could kill him. 'It would make one hell of a mess,' he observes.

Although Vermeulen now wears an old-style plastic helmet (for some reason, he thinks modern ones have a design fault), his only batting concession is to give up hooking and pulling. 'The balls that hit me both squeezed under the peak of my helmet, which you would class as a freak accident – except that now it's a freak accident which has happened twice,' he says. 'Cricket's my big love, so I decided to carry on playing and giving it a go. I try to be positive, duck and weave, and make sure it doesn't happen again.'

— SIXES AND OUT —

The promising Warwickshire batsman Graham Wagg started the 2004 season by launching Shane Warne for three successive sixes. He ended it facing a lengthy ban after a routine dope test revealed he'd taken cocaine.

— TESTING TIME —

Nothing wrong with a good, old-fashioned bunfight at pre-Test press conferences. But when there's doubt over what's *in* the buns, even seen-it-all stalwarts start to get nervous.

So it was in March 2004, when India's captain Sourav Ganguly met his country's cricket writers at the team hotel in Lahore. It was a big moment. India's first tour of Pakistan for 14 years was redolent with political symbolism and the cauldron of a Test series was seen as a way of easing tension between the two countries. Only two years earlier, a million soldiers had faced each other across the Indo-Pakistani border. The threat of all-out war had since diminished, although apparently not at Ganguly's press call.

'Could any of you please taste the cookies and tea before we serve them to Mr Ganguly,' asked a waiter casually, as though checking a cricketer's grub for poison is all part and parcel of a reporter's role. One hack, a personal friend of Sourav, agreed so long as he wasn't identified. This was accepted by all present, although the Indian skipper can hardly have had much appetite by then.

It wasn't exactly a great start, and the level of security at India's one-day practice match against a second-string Pakistan A team at Lahore's Gadaffi Stadium did little to calm nerves. This game was perhaps the most policed sports event in history, with the 300 ticket holders eyed watchfully by 2,600 policemen and 100 or so ground-security staff. This meant that each spectator could expect nine people to jump on him if he got out of line. As it turned out the entire series – which India won 2–1 – passed off without serious incident.

— KEEPING UP —

Wicket-keepers are a curious breed. They're the only players constantly involved in a match, and so arguably have more overall influence on the fate of batsmen than their team-mates. This is perhaps why, for so many years, the job was considered a specialism in itself, and any batting ability an unexpected bonus.

Not any more. Like so many aspects of modern cricket, the Australians have revolutionised attitudes by posing the awkward (if obvious) question 'Why can't great 'keepers also be great batsmen?' Being Australians, they have also provided the answer. Step forward, Adam Gilchrist.

Gilchrist has unquestionably set the standard for the world's current generation of keeper-batsmen, averaging an awesome 52.8 ahead of the 2004 India–Australia series. However, Zimbabwe's Andy Flower is not far behind, on 51.54, and Sri Lanka's Kumar Sangakkara has posted 40.28. All of them were brought up to embrace one-day cricket, a factor which has surely shaped their aggressive approach.

Fans of Alec Stewart will claim that the former glovesman was king of the dual-role 'keepers for a decade or more, but in truth Stewart was a world-class batsman required to make the most of his wicket-keeping skills in the interests of a balanced side. Without his batting returns, it's unlikely he'd have held down a regular place.

Stewart's Test average of 39.54 is comfortably ahead of 1970s stumpers such as Alan Knott – arguably England's best 'pure' wicket-keeper – who retired on 32.75, India's Farokh Engineer (31.08) and Australia's Rod Marsh (26.52). For the real plodders, you have to look further back in time to the likes of England's Herbert Strudwick, who managed a pitiful 7.93 in 28 Tests between 1910 and 1926. Juggling him between 9th and 11th in the batting order made little difference.

The table below shows how the Test averages of 'keeper-batsmen has risen over the last century:

Year	Wicket-Keepers' Batting Average
1900	16
1910	13
1920	20
1930	25
1940	23
1950	21
1960	24
1970	27
1980	24
1990	28
2000	31

— OH BROTHER —

Cricket still has a staid image, but the determined fundraisers of Hampshire's Hambledon CC – thought to be the oldest surviving club in England – are doing their bit to dispel it. Faced with a rotting and crumbling wooden pavilion, they set out to raise the final £10,000 needed for a replacement by staging their own *Big Brother*-style event, modelled on the popular reality TV series in which candidates are locked in a house rigged with cameras broadcasting to the public at large.

Being shut in a pavilion is, as any club cricketer knows, not a pleasant prospect. Ancient, sweat-encrusted socks lurk behind seats. Unclaimed underpants gently simmer beneath damp kit bags. Crusts from an egg sandwich of two seasons ago fester near the litter bin. Groin protectors – unmarked with their owner's name – seem to multiply as players turn a blind eye to their presence. You've got the picture. Perhaps even the whiff.

Hambledon (founded c1760) clearly inspires such loyalty among its players that one group agreed to be imprisoned for 48 hours, the only relief being four hours in a cage suspended high over the wicket (a shameless aping of magician David Blaine's six-week-long stunt in London in 2003). They may have earned themselves a new pavilion, but will they ever be the same again?

— HE WAS THERE —

Those who witnessed Brian Lara's record first-class innings of 501 not out for Warwickshire against Durham in 1994 will have counted themselves lucky, although probably not as lucky as one onlooker that day. The current Pakistan coach, Bob Woolmer, was there for Lara's run-fest – just as he watched the previous record holder, Hanif Mohammad, score 499 in Karachi on 11 January 1959. Woolmer was born in India and happened to be visiting Pakistan at the time with his dad.

While on the subject of Hanif – one of the true Pakistani greats who could not only keep wicket but bowl with both arms, to boot – it is a salutary lesson for cricket-trivia students that great deeds of yesteryear sometimes melt into the morass of statistics and simply get forgotten. When asked if losing his record to Lara was upsetting, Hanif sagely replied that, no, it wasn't, because 'records are there to be broken'. But, he added wistfully, 'It is a pity that for 35 years people forgot my record but remembered me when Brian Lara broke it. I got calls from England for three hours when Lara was approaching my score.' The phones must have been buzzing in the Edgbaston press box.

— DON CAP —

Four of the Test caps worn by Sir Donald Bradman have come to auction in recent years, and the latest – worn by the great man as a 21-year-old during his first trip to England in 1930 – has fetched £30,000 (£35,850 with buyer's premium) at Christie's in London. This, though, is barely a quarter of the sum supposedly paid for The Don's 1948 'Invincibles' cap.

While on the subject of cricket memorabilia, it's well worth checking your local car-boot sale for old copies of *Wisden*. An original 1876 hardback version in good nick went for £9,200 in June 2004.

— DREAM FIGURES —

In their dreams, bowlers have an endless line of 'rabbits' (the cricketing term for no-hopers) coming in to bat. However, back in the 19th century, unbalanced games such as Yatton vs The Farmers were fairly common, allowing skilled gentlemen, or professional bowlers, to gorge themselves on a very real wickets-fest.

One of the best hauls went to a Lancashire pro, left-hander Johnny Briggs, who took an astonishing 15 for 4 in a single innings while bowling for England against a 22-strong team of the Cape Mounted Riflemen at Williams Town, South Africa, in 1888–9. He finished with match figures of 27 for 23, an average of 0.85.

— FINGERED BY FOOTAGE —

The first cricketer to be given out, bowled, by a TV umpire was the West Indies' Roland Holder, playing in the 1993 Hero Cup ODI final against India. The onfield umpires couldn't decide whether the ball was deflected onto his stumps by wicket-keeper Vijay Yadav.

The match, which India won at a canter, was remarkable for two other reasons. Firstly, the West Indian collapse from 57-1 to 123 all out, thanks to an Anil Kumble spell of 6-12 in which all six wickets came in 26 balls at a cost of four runs. And secondly, the Calcutta attendance, which, at just under 100,000, was the largest crowd ever for a single day's cricket.

— SPIN WIZARDS —

England's leading post-Second World War spin bowlers are pretty much all household names. The exception (to today's generation of cricket-lovers, at least) is arguably John Henry Wardle, a Yorkshireman who in the late 1950s followed the likes of Edmund 'Ted' Peate, Robert Peel, Wilfred Rhodes and Hedley Verity to maintain his county's tradition of churning out world-class left-arm spinners.

One reason for Johnny Wardle's under-lauded reputation is that he loved playing the clown. During one match against the West Indies, he hid an opponent's bat beneath the mat wicket during a drinks interval, then pretended he had it up his jumper. In the 1953/4 West Indies Test series, he was on the field at Georgetown during a bottle-throwing incident that very nearly sparked a riot. Wardle defused the situation by picking up bottles, pretending to sip from them and doing a passable impression of a drunk.

Despite this, it was a foolish batsmen who dismissed his bowling as a joke. Although often second choice to Tony Lock, Wardle was generally considered the better performer in South Africa, Australia and the West Indies, and his Chinaman ball proved far too good for the supposedly strong South African line-up of 1956/7. Jim Laker regarded Wardle as the best slow left-armer he'd ever seen across all types of wickets and the table below certainly bears this out. Wardle has the best post-war Test average of any England spinner and his strike rate is bettered by only one man: the great Laker himself.

BEST POST-WAR ENGLAND SPINNERS TO SEPTEMBER 2004
'LA' stands for left arm; 'OB' for off-break specialists.

BOWLER	TESTS	WICKETS	AVERAGE	BEST	STRIKE RATE
DL Underwood (LA)	86	297	25.83	8–51	73.6
JC Laker (OB)	46	193	21.24	10–53	62.3
GAR Lock (LA)	49	174	25.58	7–35	75.3
FJ Titmus (OB)	53	153	32.22	7–79	98.8
JE Emburey (OB)	64	147	38.40	7–78	104.7
PH Edmonds (LA)	51	125	34.18	7–66	96.2
DA Allen (OB)	39	122	30.97	5–30	92.5
R Illingworth (OB)	61	122	31.20	6–29	97.8
PCR Tufnell (LA)	42	121	37.68	7–47	93.2
AF Giles (LA)	40	116	36.81	5–57	81.3
JH Wardle (LA)	28	102	20.39	7–36	64.6

TESTS WON BY ENGLAND'S
— LAST SIX CAPTAINS —

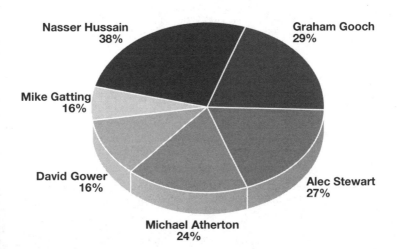

Nasser Hussain 38%

Graham Gooch 29%

Mike Gatting 16%

David Gower 16%

Alec Stewart 27%

Michael Atherton 24%

— CROWNED KING —

The souvenir mugs ordered by Warwickshire's club shop in 2003 were supposed to carry the catchphrase 'Ashley Giles, King of Spin.' They actually came out bearing the legend 'Ashley Giles, King of Spain'. While a few of Giles's critics had a field day with this (on the basis that neither statement was true), Ashley relished the moment, posing obligingly for photographers over a cuppa.

Of course, the critics are a bit quieter these days. By the end of the 2004 home season, Giles was just 65 runs away from a hallowed double of 1,000 runs and 100 wickets in Test cricket – a feat that will rank him alongside Ian Botham, Tony Greig and Trevor Bailey – and had just produced a stunning run of form against New Zealand and the West Indies.

Surely one of his fondest memories will be Brian Lara's unwise comment deriding England's supposed reliance on quick bowler Steve Harmison. 'England want to turn to him each and every time,' said Lara. 'I'm not sure he's going to last the entire summer if we do get hold of him. I don't know if they have a Plan B.' Lara discovered that there was a Plan B, and that Giles was it. The spinner took 21 wickets in three games and the Windies captain fell to him three times.

— THE COLONEL —

One of the Marylebone Cricket Club's most distinguished secretaries was Lieutenant Colonel John Stephenson, a career soldier who took the job in 1987 just as relations between MCC and the old Test and County Cricket Board were reaching a nadir. Stephenson set about re-energising his 90-odd staff, and an opening pep talk pulled no punches. 'Maybe I'm talking out of turn,' he told them, 'but why don't you take some exercise?'

Stephenson's 'watch' didn't have the best of starts. A marquee specially erected for the MCC's bicentenary ball blew down, building work on the Edrich and Compton stands fell way behind schedule, and for the first time ever members refused to accept the club's accounts. Stephenson – known universally as the Colonel – absorbed it all with nonchalant good humour.

Yet while he generally ruled with a refreshing lack of stuffiness, his occasional obsession for protocol could be both irritating and comical. According to one account, he once discovered a cricket writer interviewing the Indian captain Mohammed Azharuddin outside the windows of the Long Room. The journalist had missed a scheduled press conference and Azharuddin had nobly agreed to a quick chat.

'You know you are not allowed to conduct interviews here,' thundered the Colonel. 'Please return to the Nursery End at once.' The writer pointed out that the ground was empty, the Indian captain was agreeable and, really, what was the problem? Stephenson countered that the view of members sitting in the Long Room might be obstructed. 'But sir,' chuckled Azharuddin, 'the Long Room is totally empty.' Stephenson thought for a moment. 'Ah yes,' he said, 'but someone might come in at any moment.'

— NO CHANCE —

A young(ish) Richie Benaud once questioned Aussie all-rounder Keith Miller on what it was like to bowl at the great Sir Donald Bradman. 'Gosh, if only I could have bowled against Bradman,' sighed Richie. Miller gave him an old-fashioned look. 'Everyone has a lucky break, son,' he said. 'That was yours.'

— GENTLE TOUCH —

Sometimes a little psychology works wonders. When Shane Warne was bowling to Glamorgan batsman Darren Thomas during a 2004 county game, the Hampshire captain delivered one or two ungentlemanly comments to unnerve his young opponent. Eventually, Thomas hit back. 'I don't care what you say, Mr Warne,' he replied. 'It's a privilege for me to be on the same pitch as you.' Warne magically shut up. Thomas scored a century.

— PUFFED OUT —

How times change. Any England player caught having a crafty fag during a lunch break these days is likely to get a lecture on personal fitness and some stern advice to quit. Tobacco lovers will be heartened to know that it wasn't always so. In the 19th century, tours Down Under would sometimes conclude with a smokers-versus-non-smokers match, with each side featuring a mix of Australia and England players. The 1886–7 match at Melbourne was a classic of the genre. It was also an early example of sports sponsorship.

Prizes were offered by four major tobacco companies: 500 cigars from Jacobs, Hart & Co. for the best bowler on the smokers' team; 500 from Saqui for the smokers' top batsman; 250 cigars from Kronheimer & Co. for the highest aggregate batting score among the smokers; a further 250 for the highest individual score; and 200 cigars from White & Co., plus a trophy, for the best non-smoking bowler. Presumably the latter was supposed to make a bob by flogging the dreaded weed to his opponents.

Initially the smart money was on the smokers, who had both Johnny Briggs and George Lohman in their bowling attack. On a superlative batting wicket, however, the toss was crucial, and when the smokers lost it they were resigned to a long fielding session. Attempts to garner mental strength by taking to the field puffing cigars proved fruitless, and the day closed with the non-smokers on a healthy 422 for 2. That innings ended early on the morning of the third day on 803 for nine declared, then the highest first-class cricket score on record.

The smokers responded well at first, reaching 302 for 3 by close of play. But on the final day, they collapsed, losing their last 7 wickets for 54 runs and tottering to 135–5 in the follow-on. The match ended in a draw, with non-smoker Shrewsbury (236) and smoker Palmer (113) winning the batting prizes, and smoker Briggs (4-141) and Bates (6-73) taking bowling honours.

— GROUND RULES —

Cricket seems to have originated in medieval England, and references to a similar game, played in Kent, appear in the 13th-century household accounts of King Edward I. One theory is that the word *cricket* derives from a shepherd's 'cric' – the kind of curved stick you see in nativity plays – which was used as a bat to defend a (wicker) pasture gate, or 'wicket', from some smelly, ovoid animal bladder hurled by a bowler. That's how we got 'cric-hit'. Robin Hood is said to have bowled straight as an arrow, seam up, fast-medium. Probably.

The game expanded among the English peasantry throughout the 17th century, but no conformity of play existed until a group of distinguished gentry met at the Star and Garter pub in London's Pall Mall to draw up the first Official Laws of Cricket. These Laws remain the basis of the modern game, although officials have tinkered a little over the years. Here are the six main headings under 'Pall Mall Rules':

1   *The Game of Cricket*
2   *Laws for Bowlers – 4 Balls an Over*
3   *Laws for the Strikers, or Those that are In*
4   *Batt, Foot or Hand over the Crease*
5   *Laws for Wicket Keepers*
6   *Laws for the Umpires*

Women are thought to have played cricket since at least the 14th century, although the first recorded match wasn't until 1745, when Bramley Ladies played Hambledon Ladies. The first county women's match was between Surrey and Hampshire in 1811, when the age of players ranged from 14 to 60. Soon after this, overarm bowling was introduced by Christine Willes, who was tired of getting her bowling hand caught in her voluminous skirt while delivering underarm. Eventually, the idea caught on.

— LORD'S AND LADIES —

These are truly enlightened days. In 1999, the MCC changed its rule about having only male members. Now, for the first time in two centuries, the General Committee has its first woman: Rachel Heyhoe Flint, aka the First Lady of English cricket.

A former England captain, Heyhoe Flint has been a powerful voice for women's sport over more than four decades. She is a former hockey international, a classy golfer (she played off five) and director of PR at Wolverhampton Wanderers FC. Despite this track record, she never set out to storm male sporting bastions.

'When I started playing cricket, I didn't even realise there was an England women's team,' she told the *Daily Telegraph*. 'I've always had the attitude that if it happened, it happened. I never really had a plan.' She added: 'EW Swanton used to call it being "a cricket person", and that's what I am. I join as the MCC is investing £8.2 million in refurbishing the pavilion, but I won't be calling for frilly curtains or chintzy settees.'

Despite these words of comfort, there will be some harrumphing at Heyhoe Flint's appointment among the traditional wing of the MCC. Some members who have passed on will be doing full-skeletal doosras in the grave while those still alive (and sometimes it's hard to tell) who boast classical educations and misogynist tendencies may be tempted to quote a line from John Knox's *First Blast Of The Trumpet Against The Monstrous Regiment Of Women* (1558):

> '...Wheresoever women bear dominion, there the people must needs be disordered, living and abounding in all intemperance, given to pride, excess, and vanity; and finally, in the end, they must needs come to confusion and ruin.'

They shouldn't worry too much. Disordered living, intemperance, pride, excess, vanity, confusion and ruin – some might say it sounds like the existing model for the English cricket establishment. But let's get things in perspective. At the end of 2004 there were 18,000 members of the MCC, of which only 252 (1.4 per cent) were women. Of those 252, just 22 were full members. Given that there's currently an 18-year waiting list, the revolution is going awfully slowly. Stand easy at the bar, chaps.

— TEST BATTING RECORDS —

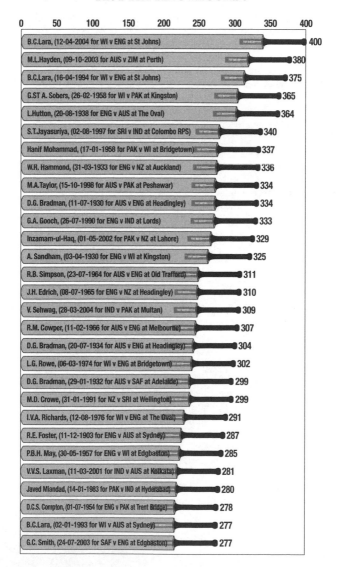

0	50	100	150	200	250	300	350	400

B.C.Lara, (12-04-2004 for WI v ENG at St Johns) — 400

M.L.Hayden, (09-10-2003 for AUS v ZIM at Perth) — 380

B.C.Lara, (16-04-1994 for WI v ENG at St Johns) — 375

G.ST A. Sobers, (26-02-1958 for WI v PAK at Kingston) — 365

L.Hutton, (20-08-1938 for ENG v AUS at The Oval) — 364

S.T.Jayasuriya, (02-08-1997 for SRI v IND at Colombo RPS) — 340

Hanif Mohammad, (17-01-1958 for PAK v WI at Bridgetown) — 337

W.R. Hammond, (31-03-1933 for ENG v NZ at Auckland) — 336

M.A.Taylor, (15-10-1998 for AUS v PAK at Peshawar) — 334

D.G. Bradman, (11-07-1930 for AUS v ENG at Headingley) — 334

G.A. Gooch, (26-07-1990 for ENG v IND at Lords) — 333

Inzamam-ul-Haq, (01-05-2002 for PAK v NZ at Lahore) — 329

A. Sandham, (03-04-1930 for ENG v WI at Kingston) — 325

R.B. Simpson, (23-07-1964 for AUS v ENG at Old Trafford) — 311

J.H. Edrich, (08-07-1965 for ENG v NZ at Headingley) — 310

V. Sehwag, (28-03-2004 for IND v PAK at Multan) — 309

R.M. Cowper, (11-02-1966 for AUS v ENG at Melbourne) — 307

D.G. Bradman, (20-07-1934 for AUS v ENG at Headingley) — 304

L.G. Rowe, (06-03-1974 for WI v ENG at Bridgetown) — 302

D.G. Bradman, (29-01-1932 for AUS v SAF at Adelaide) — 299

M.D. Crowe, (31-01-1991 for NZ v SRI at Wellington) — 299

I.V.A. Richards, (12-08-1976 for WI v ENG at The Oval) — 291

R.E. Foster, (11-12-1903 for ENG v AUS at Sydney) — 287

P.B.H. May, (30-05-1957 for ENG v WI at Edgbaston) — 285

V.V.S. Laxman, (11-03-2001 for IND v AUS at Kolkata) — 281

Javed Miandad, (14-01-1983 for PAK v IND at Hyderabad) — 280

D.C.S. Compton, (01-07-1954 for ENG v PAK at Trent Bridge) — 278

B.C.Lara, (02-01-1993 for WI v AUS at Sydney) — 277

G.C. Smith, (24-07-2003 for SAF v ENG at Edgbaston) — 277

— USELESS TOSSERS —

It can be a thankless task, being a Test skipper. Nasser Hussain recalls that during his reign he once lost ten tosses on the trot, causing much unrest among the troops. 'I always used to call heads,' he says, 'and it was a major cause of arguments in the dressing room. The bowlers would be rucking because we were in the field again. They kept urging me to call tails, but I never would.' He takes some satisfaction from the performance of his successor, Michael Vaughan, pointing out, 'Vaughany's not the best, either.'

Now, while the Laws of Probability, Averages, Standard Deviation and Large Numbers are (thankfully) not really the province of this book, there is some quality trivia interest here which will be of value to club cricket captains. Next time you're abused for losing the toss, advise your tormentors to read the formative works of Europe's leading 17th-century mathematicians, particularly Christiaan Huygens, of The Netherlands; Jakob Bernoulli, of Switzerland; and Abraham de Moivre, of France. To save you *actually* reading their stuff, let's just say they helped to establish that the chance of successfully calling heads at the toss is *always* 50–50, or evens. This rule applies whether the coin has produced 10, 100 or 10,000 heads on the trot. While it may sound obvious, it's amazing how many gamblers tell you otherwise.

The scientists realised that, while they couldn't predict the fall of a tossed coin on a one-off basis, they *could* say what the overall results would be if it was flipped hundreds or thousands of times (the Law of Large Numbers). Therefore a coin tossed 100,000 times will end up heads on roughly 50,000 occasions. The figure can't be precisely forecast, but number-crunchers get around this with something called the Law of Standard Deviation, a mathematical standard which says that there's a predictable variation in all chance events over the long term. In fact, if you were to spend a day flicking a coin 100 times every hour, on the hour, you'd find that around two-thirds of the time you'd get between 45 and 55 heads. Don't try this at home, though.

Sadly, none of the current crop of international captains have skippered 100 Tests or more, but our handy Tossers' Table below illustrates the point (we've included a couple of recently retired players for statistical purposes). Generally, the more calls a captain makes, the closer he gets to a 50 per cent success rate. This will be encouraging for Pakistan's Inzamam-ul-Haq but rather deflating for Sri Lanka's Marvin Atapattu – apart from which, we can confidently say that, as of September 2004, Nasser Hussain is a better tosser than Michael Vaughan.

Captain	Number Of Test tosses	Correct Calls	Success Rate (%)
Marvin Atapattu (Sri Lanka)	7	6	85.7
Graeme Smith (South Africa)	18	12	66.6
Heath Streak (Zimbabwe)	21	13	61.9
Stephen Fleming (New Zealand)	61	30	49.2
Steve Waugh (Australia)	57	31	54.4
Brian Lara (West Indies)	40	18	45
Nasser Hussain (England)	45	19	42.2
Sourav Ganguly (India)	39	16	41.2
Michael Vaughan (England)	19	6	31.6
Inzamam-ul-Haq (Pakistan)	7	1	14.2

— STREWTH, COBBER! —

Australian phrases such as 'bonzer', 'tinnie', 'barbie' and 'Pommie bastard' are well known and understood elsewhere. However, readers may not be familiar with slang terms on the cricket field. Caps off, then, to Richie Benaud for this invaluable guide, detailed in an interview with *The Guardian*. Being Richie, he hasn't translated – or even mentioned – any *proper* terms of abuse.

- **Gone For A Dorothy** – Used to describe any kind of failure during a game. Thus a bowler driven for six might hear deep mid-off mutter, 'That's gone for a Dorothy.' The phrase is thought to stem from a popular Australian newspaper agony aunt whose readers' letters began, 'Dear Dorothy, I'm having a problem with…' There's no truth in the rumour that most of her correspondents played for MCC.

- **An Alice** – 'That's an Alice,' you might hear a fielder observe, meaning that the ball is lost. The phrase is thought to have been inspired by a well-known ditty titled 'Alice, Where Art Thou?'

— STREWTH, COBBER! (CONT'D) —

- **Clinker** – Quite different from the British schoolboys' understanding of the word (which is connected, literally, to underpants), the Aussie term 'clinker' is merely a variation of 'bonzer' – ie something extremely good. It originates from games of marbles in which the clinker is considered to be top marble. So, if Glen McGrath beats the bat with bounce and movement, Adam Gilchrist might respond, 'That's a clinker, Glennie.'

- **Larry** – When an Australian commentator says that Ponting is 'giving it some Larry', he means that Ricky has hit the ball very hard indeed. The term refers to Larry Dooley, a much-loved hard-punching Aussie boxer.

- **Mullygrubber** – This term can be attributed to anything that crawls along the ground – like, say, an insect or weary England fielder. However, it's more usually used to describe a ball which fails to bounce properly once bowled. The English equivalent is 'daisycutter'.

— DOUBLE HEADER —

Cricketing footballers – ie players good enough to turn pro in both sports – were reasonably common in the previous century. Three, particularly, are worth a mention. It is almost unbelievable that in the space of four years Denis Compton achieved the following: 3,816 runs in a season (1947), a First Division Championship medal with Arsenal FC (1948), 562 runs in an Ashes series (1948, against Bradman's Invincibles), 406 runs with MCC in South Africa (1948/9), 300 runs against New Zealand (1949) and an FA Cup winner's medal (again with Arsenal) in 1950. Remember this the next time you hear professional footballers and cricketers grumbling about the vicissitudes of the modern game.

The second name is that of Arthur Milton, the last man to play both cricket and football for England. (Compton, incidentally, received 12 wartime football caps for his country.) Milton retired from the summer game in 1974, having amassed 32,000 first-class runs and 56 100s. He also played right wing for Arsenal and won a First Division Championship medal in 1953. In the previous season, he was awarded his England cap after coming on as substitute for Tom Finney during a 2–2 draw with Austria at Wembley. By 1958, Milton's cricketing skills had been noticed by the England selectors and he hit 104 on his debut Test, against New Zealand. Curiously, his opening partner that day was another double international, the rugby-playing Mike Smith.

Finally, there is Chris 'Iron Man' Balderstone, who not only combined careers in professional cricket and football but combined them *on the same day*. Balderstone, a handy left-arm spinner and batsman, usually sold his wicket dearly and was unlucky to feature in only two Tests, both against the awesome West Indies side of 1976. In the last of these, he went for a pair to Michael Holding and dropped Viv Richards early on. Richards went on to notch 291.

Balderstone played cricket for Yorkshire and Leicestershire and soccer for Huddersfield, Carlisle and Doncaster, later becoming a Test umpire. His finest hour as an all-round, super-fit sportsman came in September 1975, when he played a County Championship game for Yorkshire until 6:30pm, showered, changed kits and dashed to Doncaster's ground in time for a 7:30pm kick-off.

The idea that a player could today combine careers in the First Division and County Championship, let alone juggle international honours, is laughable. However it's surely only a matter of time before some reality TV show recruits 11 cricketing footballers to play 11 footballing cricketers at both sports (remember where you read this first). The footballers should certainly try to smuggle in Premiership ref Uriah Rennie, who is no mean performer with the bat.

— REAL WAG —

Tours of Pakistan are generally considered the toughest in world cricket, with heat, crowds and pitches combining to make the actual cricket seem a doddle. England have had their fair share of Pakistani pitfalls, but the biggest nosedive was unquestionably the Great Gatting Finger-Wag Affair in December 1987, during the feisty Faisalabad second Test.

The context of this contretemps lay in a simmering tension between the two sides. Pakistani captain Javed Miandad made no secret of his dislike for Gatting (who he claimed swore at him during the World Cup earlier that year). Moreover, while touring England in '87, Pakistan demanded that umpire David Constant be stood down by the Test and County Cricket Board. The TCCB refused on grounds that, according to *The Guardian*, 'we couldn't let the f*****s get away with it'. The result? Pakistan had the hump big-time.

Mix in a few other explosive ingredients from the first Test – Chris Broad refusing to walk when given out, spinner Abdul Qadir's persistent appealing and temper tantrums, Gatting's public criticism of the umpiring – and you can see why the time bomb was ticking. An additional problem was that Pakistan's players were in disgrace, their own supporters and media having not forgotten their inept World Cup display.

So we come to the end of a long, sweltering second day in Faisalabad, a day in which England had been well on top (reducing the hosts to 77–5 at one point) and Gatting had already clashed with umpire Shakoor Rana over a rejected bat-pad appeal. Rana had responded by striding down the wicket to complain about dissent and Gatting's fateful words in response were clearly picked up by the stump microphones: 'No, no, off you go. One rule for one and one rule for another.' The England skipper later claimed he hadn't intended the umpire to hear this, which seemed odd. To the Pakistani public, it also seemed a patronising, humiliating and suspiciously colonial attitude. By this point, Rana was in no mood for rapprochement. He began warning Gatting about shadows from close catchers affecting the batting side's concentration. In the penultimate over from Eddie Hemmings,

Gatting brought David Capel in from deep square leg, informing Pakistan's on-strike batsman, Salim Malik (who had his back to Capel), accordingly. On realising that Capel was too close, Gatting then waved him back. Hemmings, who had paused in his run, returned to his mark and bowled, but as the ball was in flight, Rana shouted from his square-leg position: 'Stop! Stop!' Umpire Khizar Hayat called dead ball and the verbal joust proceeded as follows:

GATTING: What's the matter?

RANA: It's unfair play.

GATTING: What's unfair play?

RANA: You're waving your hand. That's cheating. You're cheating.

Gatting points out that he has informed Malik of the fielding switch and advises Rana to get on with the game.

RANA (IN EARSHOT OF ENGLAND FIELDERS): You are a f***ing cheating c**t.

The short version of subsequent events then runs like this.

- Gatting confronts Rana, wags finger, jabs at chest.
- Photographs and footage appear around world.
- Rana refuses to continue unless Gatting apologises.
- Gatting says he will if Rana will.
- Deal brokered, but Rana backs out. Some claim Miandad, seeking to avoid defeat, persuades Rana to stand firm for honour of Pakistan.
- Entire third day lost.
- England players sign statement of support for skipper.
- Foreign Office orders tour manager Peter Lush to solve impasse 'at any cost'.
- Gatting produces tatty scrap of scrawled paper saying sorry 'for the bad language used'.
- Game continues. Match drawn. England lose series 1–0.

— THE DUCKWORTH-LEWIS (RAIN) RULE —

Oh Lor! Before explaining how this mathematical beauty works, it's worth setting out Agnew's Law on the Duckworth-Lewis method:

1   Never pretend to understand it. Only two people do, and you're not one of them.

2   Never scoff at it. Even the most contrary professional cricketer accepts that it's the best system going.

3   Never ask anyone to explain it, especially if there's some paint nearby that you can watch drying instead.

The Duckworth-Lewis (Rain) Rule is designed to revise target scores fairly in limited-over games disrupted by the weather. Its aim is to maintain the balance of a match right through any suspension and, in order to achieve this, each side is allocated 'resources' in the form of overs remaining or wickets in hand. If a team batting first loses overs due to rain, its opponents will often find themselves facing a higher total than was actually scored. Similarly, a team going in second might find that their target has been adjusted downwards.

An important factor is the point at which rain came. If it piddles down late in an innings – especially when wickets are in hand – the loss of resources is deemed far greater than if the break comes early. Obviously, a team on 150–1 with ten overs left is well placed to unleash a run-fest. However, the same side forced to come off between, say, the 15th and 25th overs would probably not have been looking to thrash the bowling. Its loss of resources would therefore be much less.

All clear? Never mind. Just take a look at the following table. It's an abbreviated version of the one used by scorers, so just be thankful for that! As most international one-dayers are 50 overs per innings, the calculations are tailored accordingly.

OVERS LEFT	0 WKTS LOST	2 WKTS LOST	5 WKTS LOST	8 WKTS LOST
50	100.0	83.8	49.5	16.4
40	90.3	77.6	48.3	16.4
30	77.1	68.2	45.7	16.4
20	58.9	54.0	40.0	16.4
10	34.1	32.5	27.5	14.9

Let's say the Dunstable Ducklings are playing the Stratford Strollers. The Ducklings bat first and score 280. The Strollers reach 130 for 2 after 30 overs, whereupon the heavens open. At this point there are 20 overs remaining and two wickets down. The table reveals that 54 per cent of resources remain.

Time spent off the field means that the Strollers' innings is reduced to 40 overs. Play resumes with ten overs remaining and, still, two wickets down. The table therefore indicates that 32.5 per cent of resources remain.

Now, we know – and sit up straight there at the back – that the total resources lost is 54 per cent minus 32.5 per cent, which leaves 21.5 per cent. The Strollers have 78.5 per cent (that's 100 minus 21.5) of available resources, compared with the Ducklings' 100 per cent. The Strollers' new target is therefore 78.5 per cent of 280, ie 219.8 – or, revised to the nearest whole number, 220.

That's the nuts of it, although the principle is applied slightly differently for a rain-break affecting the first batting team. Moving quickly on, trivia fiends will need to note that Frank Duckworth is a consultant statistician and editor of the Royal Statistical Society's monthly newsletter, while Tony Lewis is a lecturer in mathematical subjects at the University of the West of England. The pair teamed up after a 1994 statistics conference where Duckworth presented a paper on target correction. Lewis later invited his students to apply it to cricket.

— CHATTY BRETT —

It was Steve Waugh who first recognised the huge commercial potential for Australian Test players in India, although even he may balk at the news that Brett Lee is being taught to speak Hindi. Even so, Waugh might consider urging Adam Gilchrist to tone down the straight-talking interview style he adopted on the eve of the 2004 Test series between the two countries.

Gilchrist stopped short of saying, 'We Aussies are gonna ruthlessly milk you sucker Indians for every last rupee,' but only just short. What he *actually* said was, 'I think we're all pretty aware of the opportunities now. There's so much easy money out there, smash-and-grab money, where you do work that is easy and you get well paid for it.' Someone had better warn the Board of Control for Cricket in India that Gilchrist is eyeing their 2.2 billion rupee (£25 million) war chest.

— BIG TONE —

The tallest men ever to play first-class cricket are Anthony Allom, a former Charterhouse School and Surrey IIs player who turned out for the Free Foresters against Oxford University in June 2003, and Will 'Lofty' Jefferson, currently of Essex. Both are just two inches short of 7', the kind of batsmen for whom bouncers 'get up nicely'. Allom, by the way, can boast a pedigree to go with his undoubted power: his father Maurice Allom was a handy new ball bowler for Surrey and England between the wars.

This pair's nearest rivals in the beanpole-batsmen department are JDF Larter, of Northamptonshire IIs; Nigel Paul, formerly of Warwickshire (he also bowled left-arm fast/medium); the late CG Ford, who played for MCC in 1932; and PH Ford (no relation), who turned out for Gloucestershire before World War I. All of them topped the 6'7" mark.

According to *The Cricketer International*, at least 100 players of 6'3" or more (of which I am one!) have played the first-class game. *The Cricketer* also records that the heaviest player of all time is one W Foulkes, of Derbyshire, who weighed in at a colossal 25 stone, 'at least'. He was also a goalkeeper, presumably of the ilk that doesn't notice centre-forwards bouncing off them.

Cricket supporters rarely break into choruses of 'Who Ate All The Pies?' but historical candidates for this tuneful jibe would surely have included the 22 stone 10lb CH Gausden, who turned out for Sussex in the mid-19th century, and even old WG Grace himself, whose weight apparently fluctuated between 14 stone 8lb and 18 stone. Pride of place, though, must go to George Brown – another Sussex player of Victorian vintage – who tipped the scale at 18 stone despite burning up lots of calories fathering 17 children.

Among the lightest players ever to grace the first-class game is John Wisden, who at one point in his early career was a featherweight 7 stone.

— IRISH CHEER —

Heard the one about the Irishmen, Englishmen, West Indians and Zimbabweans? The short version is that the Irish beat reigning county champions Surrey in the 2004 Cheltenham & Gloucester Trophy, saw off the West Indies the same year to successfully chase 293 and, in 2003, humbled the Zimbabweans by ten wickets. Opponents who think Irish cricket is a joke should tread carefully.

— BARRY THE BAT —

Barry Richards' career Test record for the Springboks reads as follows:

OPPONENTS: SA VS AUSTRALIA, 1969–70	1ST INNINGS	2ND INNINGS
1ST TEST	29	32
2ND TEST	140	Did not bat
3RD TEST	65	35
4TH TEST	81	126

Younger readers may wonder why a man who scored 508 runs in his debut series, at an average of 72.57, played only four times for his country – especially when his opponents in the series concerned included Australians of the calibre of Bill Lawry, Ian Chappell, Doug Walters, Ian Redpath, Keith Stackpole, Johnny Gleeson and Graham McKenzie.

Richards was, of course, a sporting victim of South Africa's reviled apartheid regime. Just as he blossomed into one of cricket's natural geniuses, South Africa's politics were making the Springboks (now known as the Proteas) a pariah of world sport. By the time Pretoria hauled itself back into the 20th century under FW de Clerk and Nelson Mandela, it was all far too late for Barry Richards.

It seems absurd to complain about his loss to international cricket alongside the privations of black South Africans, but, from a sporting point of view, complain we must. Sir Donald Bradman once described him as 'the world's best ever right-handed opener', and anyone who saw Richards murder the Australian attack in his second Test would surely agree. Just after lunch that day, he and Graeme Pollock produced the greatest hour-long batting spree ever seen in South Africa, helping their side to 622–9.

Older Hampshire fans sigh wistfully at the recollection of Richards and the great West Indian Gordon Greenidge strolling out to open for the county in the late 1960s. Together they tormented opposition bowlers, whatever the speed or style. Richards totalled 2,395 runs in the 1968 county championship, and on nine occasions in his first-class career he scored a century before lunch.

He was perhaps at his peak while playing Sheffield Shield cricket in Perth for South Australia in 1970/1 against a Western Australia attack that included Dennis Lillee, Garth McKenzie and England's Tony Lock. That day, it was virtually impossible to bowl anything at Richards; in three sessions, unbeaten, he scored an astonishing 325 runs. If he had graced more Test matches, few batting records would have been safe.

— SPORTING HIGH —

Whatever the sport, high humidity is the player's worst nightmare since it reduces the cooling effect of sweating. Just ask Adam Hollioake, who, reflecting on a 1998 ICC Champions' Trophy game in the steamy atmosphere of Dhaka, told one reporter, 'I haven't actually done it, but I felt like I'd smoked ten joints.'

— ENOUGH SAID —

Ahead of the 2004 ICC Champions' Trophy in England, Shane Warne had a pop at Marcus Trescothick, claiming in a newspaper column that the Somerset opener's technique wasn't adaptable enough. Shane reckoned a spell back in county cricket would do 'Banger' some good.

'I did give Warne's comments slight consideration at the time, but not when we played the Aussies on Tuesday,' Trescothick said later. 'Everybody has got their views, and they are entitled to them, but I was a bit surprised about it at the time.' What he actually meant was, 'It might be hard to dislike Shane Warne, but it's worth the effort.'

Oh yes, that game against the Aussies. Wasn't that the one in which Trescothick and Michael Vaughan put on 141 for the first wicket and Banger smacked 81 off 88 balls, including four successive fours in one over from Glenn McGrath, and Australia were comprehensively trounced with 3.5 overs left, to miss out once again on the ICC Trophy?

Thought so.

— 100 CLUB —

In January 1901, New South Wales supporters must have been dreading a visit from South Australia. Only the previous month their side had been whipped at Adelaide, and an encore seemed on the cards. Imagine their surprise, then, when they turned to the sports pages of the Sydney *Daily Telegraph* to discover not only that the visitors were all out in their first innings for 157, but that the NSW boys performed as follows:

Iredale	c Jarvis (AH) b Travers	118
Trumper	b Jarvis (F)	70
Noble	c Giffen b Matthews	153
Hopkins	c Jarvis (AH) b Travers	27
Gregory	b Jarvis (F)	168
Duff	st Jarvis (AH) b Travers	119
Poidevin	not out	140
Howard	c Bailey b Matthews	64
Kelly	c Hill b Hack	34
McBeth	c Walkeley b Bailey	7
Marsh	lbw b Travers	1
	Extras	17
	Total	**918**

This really was revenge super-sized. Iredale's 118 took 135 minutes, Duff's century took under two hours, Noble's was posted in 160 minutes, Gregory's in 165 minutes and Poidevin – a dreadful plodder in his first big match – took all of 210 minutes (although he did finish unbeaten). South Australia batted again and, mercifully, were skittled out for 156, giving their hosts victory by an implausible innings and 605 runs.

Marsh did all the damage with the ball, taking ten wickets in the match, but it is fitting that a McBeth appears in the New South Wales line-up. In the Shakespearean tragedy *Macbeth*, the lead character stares at an imaginary dagger as he walks to murder King Duncan; 'I have thee not, yet I see thee still,' he wails. South Australia must have felt the same about the scorecard.

— ALL RIGHT JACK —

The world record for the number of catches held by any player in a single Test match is 11 – all pouched by England wicket-keeper Jack Russell at Johannesburg in the 1995/6 series against South Africa. Russell, who played 54 tests and 40 ODIs for his country, was unquestionably one of England's greatest post-war 'keepers, but he's best remembered among team-mates for some eccentric habits on tour. These included hanging a tea bag on his peg in the dressing room (it was usually used more than once) and washing all his own kit, which would be suspended off hotel lampshades to dry.

— RELATIVE VALUES —

Only one father-and-son pair have represented the same country in ODIs: Chris and Lance Cairns of New Zealand. Don and Derek Pringle can lay a similar claim, but Don appeared for East Africa and Derek for England.

The only time three sets of brothers have appeared in a World Cup match was in the 2003 game between Zimbabwe and Namibia. Zimbabwe's side included Grant and Andy Flower, while Namibia fielded Deon and Bjorn Kotze and Louis and Sarel Burger.

In case you were wondering, the first twins to play together in a Test match were Rosemary and Elizabeth Signal, who appeared for New Zealand against England in 1984.

— LAST EFFORT —

One Day International cricket was invented by accident when the first four days of an Australia-vs-England Test match at Melbourne in 1971 were lost to rain. Both sides agreed to a one-day unofficial thrash on the final day, which Australia won.

The shortest Test match on record was the encounter between Sri Lanka and India at Colombo in 1996. Just 50 minutes of play were possible.

— GREAT BOTCH-UPS AND BLUNDERS —

SOUTH AFRICA VS SRI LANKA, 2002/3 WORLD CUP, DURBAN
This was the earth-shaking momma of them all. South Africa had been chasing a target of 269 thanks to a magnificent 152-run partnership by Marvan Atapattu (124 off 129 balls) and Aravinda de Silva (73). Rain reduced this total to 229 under the Duckworth-Lewis method, and after the usual scares and shenanigans a solid stand of 63 between skipper Shaun Pollock and Mark Boucher put the Proteas on the brink of victory. And that's precisely where they stayed.

As the South African innings wore on, 12th man Nicky Boje was despatched to make sure that Boucher and his new partner, Lance Klusener, understood what was required. Computer printouts of Duckworth-Lewis calculations are available to teams on a ball-by-ball basis, so this should have been obvious. Whether Boje wasn't given a proper chance to explain (South African officials later claimed the umpires had shooed him away) or whether his team-mates simply didn't understand that the D-L formula produced the target for a *tie* – not the win they needed – isn't clear. Either way, it was a shocker.

With rain falling once more, Boucher realised he had to get on with the job. When he smashed a six off the penultimate ball of Muralitharan's over, taking his team to 229, he believed the job was done. Cautious and watchful, he blocked out the final delivery of the 45th over rather than push for an easy single. At that point the rain got heavier, the covers came on, the match was abandoned and each side was given two points for a tie. South Africa had ejected themselves from their own World Cup.

SOUTH AFRICA VS AUSTRALIA, 1999 WORLD CUP SEMI-FINAL, EDGBASTON

Oh Lordy! This one was even worse for the Proteas, since it cost them a place in the final itself. Australia had been bustled out for a very gettable 213 and South Africa were coasting on 48 for 0 when a combination of Shane Warne and the Panic Button reduced them to 61 for 4.

With time ticking on, Lance Klusener (him again) bludgeoned 31 off 15 balls to put his side within one run of victory, with three balls left. He drove for a single, but his non-striking partner Alan Donald responded with a passable impression of a rabbit caught in headlights, dropped his bat and was left stranded. The incredulous Aussies celebrated with a bonzer 'pile-on' and went on to win the Cup. It's some small consolation for South Africa that this game is regarded by many as the greatest one-day match ever.

— GREAT BOTCH-UPS AND BLUNDERS (CONT'D) —

WEST INDIES VS ENGLAND, FOURTH TEST, PORT OF SPAIN, 1967/8

There's nothing wrong with forcing a result, but when Garry Sobers declared on 92–2 in the Windies' second innings, he was far too generous to an England side needing 215 runs in two and three-quarter hours, an asking rate of less than four an over.

Given that the wicket had yielded 930 runs from the first two innings, and that the tourists' team included Edrich, Cowdrey, Barrington, Graveney and D'Oliveira, this was not Sobers' greatest tactical decision. In the event, Boycott played a crucial anchor role (80 not out) while Cowdrey (71) and Edrich (29) secured a seven-wicket win – and the series – for England.

AUSTRALIA VS WEST INDIES, THIRD TEST, MELBOURNE 1988/9

At the end of the fourth day, with the West Indies heading for a lead of 400 runs, Steve Waugh had the *really* dumb idea of bowling a bouncer at Patrick 'Patto' Patterson. The Aussies had enough to worry about with Marshall, Ambrose and Walsh steaming in on the back of a big score. Making Patto unnecessarily cross (he was then just about the fastest bowler in the world) really shouldn't have been in the game plan.

And cross he was! So cross that he stormed into the Australian dressing room to mention in passing that he was going to kill them all on the final day. Fortunately, no guts were spilled, only wickets. Patterson took 5 for 39 in 15.1 bowel-loosening overs, adding to his 4 for 49 in the first innings. Australia were all out for 114, lost the match by 285 runs and went on to lose the series 3–1.

AUSTRALIA VS WEST INDIES, 1993 WORLD SERIES FIRST FINAL, SYDNEY

What part of 'Don't provoke them, stupid!' do you reckon Aussies can't understand? As Curtly Ambrose was getting into his stride, Australia's number three Dean Jones complained to the umpires about his white wristbands. 'He was definitely trying some form of camouflage,' Jones said later. 'I didn't think much of it at the time.'

Unfortunately for the Aussies, Curtly thought quite a lot of it and decided he was mightily brassed off. With a run-up now distinctly purposeful, he annihilated their batting in 9.3 overs, taking 5 for 32 and holding a crucial catch off Carl Hooper to dismiss the dangerous Allan Border. West Indies won the match by 25 runs. Just possibly, Dean lost it.

INDIA VS AUSTRALIA, 2000/1 SECOND TEST, KOLKATA

You can't really blame Steve Waugh for this one. At the time, his decision to enforce the follow-on seemed sensible; India were 274 behind and looking thoroughly demoralised. Then it all went pear-shaped. VVS Laxman waded into an Aussie attack comprising McGrath, Kasprowicz, Gillespie and Warne to score an awesome 281, while at the other end Dravid helped himself to 180.

By the time India declared, on 657–7, it was the Australians' turn to look ragged. They were shot out for just 212, with Harbhajan Singh taking 6 for 73, to give India the unlikeliest of wins by 171 runs. For Waugh it was the bitterest of pills; from 1–0 up, the tourists went on to lose the rubber 2–1, and Waugh never did achieve his Holy Grail of winning a series in India.

ENGLAND VS AUSTRALIA, 1993 SECOND TEST, LORDS

Talking of Holy Grails, it is a bizarre truth that former England skipper Michael Atherton never scored a century against Australia in England and never got his name on the Honours Board at Lords (you need either five wickets or a century). Yet, but for a moment's indecision – no, let's call it a botch-up – he would have achieved both ambitions at a stroke.

Atherton, one of England's most reliable post-war openers, was on 97 when he pushed the ball for what looked a certain three. His partner, Mike Gatting, called for the third run, but then sent Athers back. Atherton slipped and was two yards adrift, on all fours, when Ian Healy shattered his stumps and his hopes. There apparently wasn't much left of the England dressing-room door that day, either.

— RABBIT'S REVENGE —

Insurance companies are well used to their clients' weird and wonderful misfortunes, but the claim form submitted by Wiltshire's Devizes Cricket Club in August 2004 must have been an absolute cracker. Essentially, it would have read as follows:

- Club volunteers light bonfire after ground maintenance session. They pour on paraffin to get things going.

- Rabbit hiding among dead branches dashes out with tail on fire.

- Volunteers conduct search to find rabbit. Fail, shrug and carry on.

- Nearby groundsman's hut starts to smoulder, then bursts into flames. Volunteers realise that blazing rabbit hid in hut.

- Hut engulfed by fire. £60,000 worth of maintenance equipment destroyed, including mowers, wheelbarrows and electrical connections to the club's new electronic scoreboard.

Ground committee chairman Richard Read said, 'The rabbit must have had paraffin poured over it and caught fire at the same time. We ran to see where it had got to but couldn't find it. We can only imagine that it bolted inside the hut, because shortly afterwards it started burning. The fire spread to the whole place in a few minutes, and there was no chance of getting anything out.'

— CRICKET AND SEX —

Getting women more involved in sport has become a perennial quest for the advertising industry for two reasons: they're a lucrative, untapped market for kit manufacturers, and they're not half as mean as blokes when they go shopping. Mindful that TV executives want what advertisers want, sports administrators are doing their level best to 'sex up' their brands. Hence the bizarre suggestion from FIFA President Sepp Blatter that women footballers should wear shorter, tighter shorts because they'd attract bigger crowds.

You might think that cricket is above all this...and you'd be wrong. A columnist on the Indiatimes website, Shah Purchit, believes that the Board of Cricket Control for India should take the lead. 'I wonder if women's cricket would become more popular if the dress code were changed,' he muses. 'Women's tennis is a very popular sport. Even women's hockey is much looked forward to. Yet women's cricket is hardly watched at all. Why?'

He suggests that if women players were to wear short skirts instead of trousers, the 'popularity polls…would take a definite upward swing', adding that 'almost every game has progressed from long pants to half pants to short skirts to micro minis to just beachwear.' Why stop at beachwear, though? What about a 'Thongs 'n' Topless' Women's Twenty20 League? That should keep the St John Ambulance Brigade busy with defibrillators.

— FIELDING FOLLIES —

Who'd have thought it? The only Test batsman ever to have been given out for 'obstructing the field' was Sir Len Hutton, playing against South Africa at the Oval in 1951. At that time, Hutton was at the peak of his powers, having averaged 88.83 in the 1950/1 Test series against Australia.

The only batsman dismissed for obstruction in the history of ODIs is former Pakistan captain Rameez Raja, who tried to avoid a run-out by using his bat to deflect what otherwise could have been a direct hit on the stumps. He had tried to nick a single off the last ball of an innings against England at Karachi in 1987.

Curiously, Raja was involved in another controversial fielding incident in January that same year, again against England. While batting at Perth, he was caught off a no-ball but, failing to hear the umpire's call, left his crease to return to the pavilion. He was given out 'run out' by the square-leg umpire.

Interestingly, only two Englishmen have ever been given out for handling the ball in Test matches: Graham Gooch and Michael Vaughan.

— HIGH DRAMA —

If close-run things are your bag, then always book your ticket early for a New Zealand versus Australia One Day International encounter. The Kiwis have secured one-run victories against their neighbours on three occasions (1981, 1988 and 1990, all in Australia). An analysis of international one-run victories since 1976 also reveals the astonishing statistic that, between them, these two countries have been involved in 13 of the 16 on record.

The stats for one-wicket victories are a little less clear, Australia having beaten the Kiwis by this margin on just one occasion. However, one or other of the two teams has been involved in 8 of the 25 results on record. Mathematically speaking, if you like a skin-of-the-teeth, nail-biting run chase, then aim to watch England, Pakistan or the West Indies who between them have played a part in 20 of the 25 one-wicket wins.

What all this says about the cricket – other than that some sides enjoy torturing supporters – is anyone's guess. The breakdown is below, followed by the wheres and whens.

Country	Number Of ODI Wins By 1 Run	Number Of ODI Losses By 1 Run
Australia	4	4
New Zealand	4	4
India	2	2
South Africa	2	2
West Indies	1	1
Pakistan	1	1
Sri Lanka	1	1
Zimbabwe	1	1
England	0	0
Bangladesh	0	0

Country	Number Of ODI Wins By 1 Wicket	Number Of ODI Losses By 1 Wicket
West Indies	8	5
Pakistan	4	6
England	4	3
Zimbabwe	3	2
Australia	2	1
New Zealand	2	5
India	1	3

COUNTRY	NUMBER OF ODI WINS BY 1 WICKET	NUMBER OF ODI LOSSES BY 1 WICKET
Sri Lanka	1	0
Bangladesh	0	1
South Africa	0	0

ONE-RUN VICTORY MARGINS IN ONE DAY INTERNATIONALS

- **Sri Lanka beat Australia,** 22 February 2004, Second ODI, Rangiri Dambulla Stadium , Rangiri;

- **Australia beat Zimbabwe,** 4 February 2001, 12th match, Carlton Series, the WACA, Perth;

- **South Africa beat England,** 26 Jan 2000, third match, Standard Bank Triangular, Newlands, Cape Town;

- **Zimbabwe beat New Zealand,** 4 March 1998 , third ODI, Lancaster Park, Christchurch;

- **South Africa beat New Zealand,** 11 December 1997, fifth match, Carlton and United Series, Bellerive Oval, Hobart;

- **Australia beat South Africa,** 8 April 1994, fifth ODI, Springbok Park, Bloemfontein;

- **India beat Sri Lanka,** 25 July 1993, first ODI, Khettarama Stadium, Colombo;

- **Australia beat India,** 1 March 1992, 12th match, Benson & Hedges World Cup, BCG, Woolloongabba, Brisbane;

- **Pakistan beat West Indies,** 21 October 1991, fourth match, Wills Trophy, Sharjah CA Stadium, Sharjah;

- **New Zealand beat Australia,** 18 December 1990, second match, Benson & Hedges World Series Cup, Bellerive Oval, Hobart;

- **India beat New Zealand,** 6 March 1990, fourth match, Rothmans Triangular, Basin Reserve, Wellington;

- **West Indies beat Australia,** 13 December 1988, third match, Benson & Hedges World Series, SCG, Sydney;

— HIGH DRAMA (CONT'D) —

- **New Zealand beat Australia**, 3 January 1988, second match, Benson & Hedges World Series, The WACA, Perth;

- **Australia beat India**, 9 October 1987, third match Reliance World Cup, Chidambaram Stadium, Chepauk, Madras;

- **New Zealand beat Australia**, 13 January 1981, 12th match, Benson & Hedges World Series Cup, SCG, Sydney;

- **New Zealand beat Pakistan**, 16 October 1976, first ODI, Jinnah Stadium, Sialkot.

ONE-WICKET VICTORY MARGINS IN ONE DAY INTERNATIONALS
- **West Indies beat Bangladesh**, 15 May 2004, first ODI, Arnos Vale Ground, Kingstown, St Vincent;

- **India beat New Zealand**, 11 January 2003, sixth ODI, Eden Park, Auckland;

- **Zimbabwe beat India**, 7 March 2002, first ODI, Nahar Singh Stadium, Faridabad;

- **West Indies beat Zimbabwe**, 13 January 2001, second match, Carlton Series, BCG, Woolloongabba, Brisbane;

- **Zimbabwe beat New Zealand**, 7 January 2001, third ODI, Eden Park, Auckland;

- **Zimbabwe beat India**, 8 December 2000, third ODI, Barkatullah Khan Stadium, Pal Road, Jodhpur;

- **England beat Zimbabwe**, 18 February 2000, second ODI, Queens Sports Club, Bulawayo;

- **Sri Lanka beat England**, 23 January 1999, eighth match, Carlton Series, Adelaide Oval, Adelaide;

- **West Indies beat England**, 1 April 1998, second ODI, Kensington Oval, Bridgetown, Barbados;

- **West Indies beat New Zealand**, 26 March 1996, first ODI, Sabina Park, Kingston, Jamaica;

- **Australia beat West Indies,** 1 January 1996, fifth match World Series, SCG, Sydney;

- **New Zealand beat Pakistan,** 17 December 1995, second ODI, Lancaster Park, Christchurch;

- **Australia beat New Zealand,** 21 March 1993, second ODI, Lancaster Park, Christchurch;

- **West Indies beat Pakistan,** 17 October 1991, first match, Wills Trophy, Sharjah Stadium, Sharjah;

- **England beat West Indies,** 23 May 1991, first ODI, Edgbaston, Birmingham;

- **Pakistan beat West Indies,** 16 October 1987, ninth match, Reliance World Cup, Gadaffi Stadium, Lahore;

- **England beat Pakistan,** 25 May 1987, third ODI, Edgbaston, Birmingham;

- **Pakistan beat Australia,** 2 January 1987, third match, Benson & Hedges challenge, the WACA, Perth;

- **Pakistan beat India,** 18 April 1986, final, Australasia Cup, Sharjah Stadium, Sharjah;

- **Pakistan beat New Zealand,** 7 December 1984, fourth ODI, Ibn-e-Qasim Bagh Stadium, Multan;

- **West Indies beat Pakistan,** 28 January 1984, 11th match, Benson & Hedges World Series, Adelaide Oval, Adelaide;

- **West Indies beat Pakistan,** 16 January 1982, 13th match, Benson & Hedges World Series, BCG, Woolloongabba, Brisbane;

- **New Zealand beat West Indies,** 6 February 1980, first ODI, Lancaster Park, Christchurch;

- **West Indies beat Pakistan,** 11 June 1975, eighth match, World Cup, Edgbaston, Birmingham;

- **England beat West Indies,** 5 September 1973, first ODI, Headingley, Leeds.

— WALK-ON PART —

When Don Bradman strode out of the pavilion gates at the Oval on 14 August 1948, he was cheered to the wicket by both the crowd and the England team. This was The Don's final innings in the Old Country, and as cricket-lovers knew – and know – he needed just four runs to clinch a Test average of 100.

When Bradman was bowled for a duck, it was widely assumed his eyesight had been affected by tears. He later dismissed the suggestion as 'a great exaggeration', and the man who got his wicket, Eric Hollies, readily agreed. Hollies' first ball was a standard leg break, but he followed it with a devastating googly that took the off bail. Bradman was promptly given a standing ovation, to the chagrin of the bowler. 'My best bloody ball of the season,' he told a fielder, 'and they're clapping *him*.'

— GETTING TO GRIPS —
THREE CLASSIC BOWLING GRIPS FOR MEDIUM PACERS

Inswing grip

Outswing grip

Offcutter grip

Inswing And Outswing Bowling

Getting a cricket ball to swerve, or 'swing', in the air depends largely on seam position at the bowler's point of release. As long as the seam stays vertical, and the shiniest side of the ball is on the outside of the planned curve *en route* to the batsman, the ball should swing in the direction the seam is angled. For the outswinger, therefore, the ball should be gripped with the first two fingers, close together on the seam, with the side of the thumb acting as a support – again, on the seam – underneath. The bowler then moves the seam to point at first slip. For the inswinger, the seam is moved to point at leg slip.

Note: A ball's swingability is affected by several other factors: whether the action is side-on or chest-on, the height of the arm at release, the follow-through position of the hand, the speed of delivery and, especially, the atmospheric conditions. Give a swing bowler moist, warm and humid conditions and he's like a pig in a sewage plant.

The Offcutter

Effectively a fast off-break, the offcutter can be a devilish delivery – especially from bowlers whose stock ball moves the opposite way (ie away from the right-handed batsman). The ball is gripped with the index finger placed along the top of the seam, the thumb along the bottom and the middle finger roughly between the two. At the moment of delivery, the fingers are whipped down the side of the ball, the thumb passes over the top and the ball fizzes wickedly off the pitch between bat and pad to demolish middle stump. That's the theory, anyhow.

— SWEET SIXTEEN —

The youngest player ever to score a Test half-century was India's Sachin Tendulkar, who was 16 years and 214 days when he knocked 59 at Faisalabad during the second Test between India and Pakistan in 1989.

— WORLD FIRST —

The first man to play in both the cricket and rugby World Cups was Dr Rudie van Vuuren of Namibia. Van Vuuren, an opening medium-pacer and speedy fly-half, was named in his country's squad for both 2003 tournaments. Despite describing himself as 'not that good at cricket', he was good enough to return 5–43 off ten overs in a pool game against England, taking the wickets of Michael Vaughan, Nick Knight, Craig White, Ronnie Irani and Andy Caddick.

— CRICKET OLYMPIANS —

Of all the unlikely sporting events to feature at the Olympics (and there have been a few), a cricket match between England and France is right up there in the Bizarre Top Ten. It happened in August 1900, when a Great Britain XI in the shape of the Devon and Somerset Wanderers Cricket Club played France at the Paris Olympics.

Skimpy details of this encounter appear in an old school magazine unearthed from the archives of Blundell's School, at Tiverton, Devon. The piece was apparently written by a member of the Great Britain team, a former Old Blundellian, who bemoaned the fact that the planned three-match series was shortened to a single game because 'no Frenchman could be persuaded to play more than once'. The match, staged in a new 20,000-seat velodrome, was witnessed by only 20 or so bored and baffled gendarmes, and the French participants were accused of being 'too excitable to enjoy the game'.

That last criticism is a bit rich given that, having humiliated the French team (which in any case included several British ex-pats), the GB party embarked on some 'excitable' celebrations of their own – so much so that one of their drivers had to ride back to the team's lodgings inside the coach, as he was so 'excited' by victory. The other driver was obviously in a similar state: he crashed the coach, causing minor injury to one 17-stone cricketer.

Being well-brought-up chaps, the Devon and Somerset Wanderers never did lay claim to being Olympic champions. They were happy enough with their silver medals (the French received bronze) and their souvenir models of the Eiffel Tower. If anyone asked, they modestly referred to the Paris 'Test' as an 'exhibition match'. Two of the team went on to win Somerset caps: Montagu Toller, who played six times for the county, and Alfred Bowerman, who played twice.

— SHORT BOWLERS —

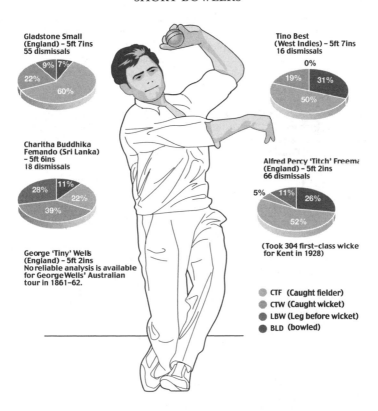

Gladstone Small
(England) – 5ft 7ins
55 dismissals

9% 7%
22%
60%

Tino Best
(West Indies) – 5ft 7ins
16 dismissals

0%
19% 31%
50%

Charitha Buddhika
Femando (Sri Lanka)
– 5ft 6ins
18 dismissals

11%
28%
22%
39%

Alfred Percy 'Titch' Freema
(England) – 5ft 2ins
66 dismissals

5% 11% 26%
52%

(Took 304 first-class wicke
for Kent in 1928)

George 'Tiny' Wells
(England) – 5ft 2ins
No reliable analysis is available
for George Wells' Australian
tour in 1861–62.

- ● CTF (Caught fielder)
- ● CTW (Caught wicket)
- ● LBW (Leg before wicket)
- ● BLD (bowled)

— WIRED UP —

It was a good win, no doubt of that, but South Africa's opening batsman Andrew Hudson got a little carried away as the West Indies were skittled for 136 in the 17th match of the 1992 World Cup in Christchurch. The jubilant Hudson uprooted a stump and galloped off to the pavilion, only to find that his prized memento included a miniature TV camera and ten metres of cable ripped from beneath the pitch.

— LIGHTEN UP —

Laws covering poor light during matches have always been a touch controversial. When visibility deteriorates, the umpires are supposed to confer and may offer the batting side a chance to walk off. If the batsmen 'take the light', the umpires whip out their meters and note down the reading. Conditions must then improve before play resumes.

It's not quite clear – to many cricket supporters, at least – why batsmen are put in charge of proceedings. They may be at the sharp end of the fast bowling, but at least they know which direction the ball is coming from. Fielders, however, might find it incredibly difficult to see the ball in flight. Cries of 'It's coming your way!' from team-mates are not always entirely helpful.

This problem has recently been addressed to some extent, because if floodlights are used to supplement natural light in ordinary 'day' games, fielders can be given the option to come off. Of course, while umpires are expected to consider the physical safety of players, the players themselves are more concerned with tactical advantage. Two recent England matches illustrate the point. On the third day of the 2002 Auckland Test, Nasser Hussain's men came off at 12–3, even though some of the fielders were still sporting sunglasses. Yet, on the fourth day, New Zealand's Craig McMillan and Nathan Astle, having been offered the light at 5:30pm, carried on for 90 minutes after the official close of play and an incredible 40 minutes after Auckland's official lighting-up time. They were aided by the use of floodlights – a dubious advantage against the red ball.

The Kiwis' reasoning was simple: they were marmalising the England bowling and could therefore hardly be in mortal peril. The visitors, in contrast, were doing all they could to slow the over rate, clearly dischuffed at a lead stretching above 300. For both sides, the question of poor light was principally tactical, although Hussain twice engaged the umpires in discussions about the danger to his fielders. Delaying tactics might have been at the forefront of his mind, but he had a point; England's substitute fielder Usman Afzaal had just let a potential catch at fine leg go for six because he was covering his head with his hands. New Zealand eventually won by 78 runs to draw the three-Test series 1–1.

Hussain insisted afterwards that he didn't want to be labelled 'a whingeing English captain', but pointed out that 'some of our boys were struggling to see the ball'. He added, 'I mentioned that to [umpire Srinivas Venkataraghavan], and he fully agreed with me and said, "Yeah, it is difficult, but at no time in the history of the game has any side been taken off fielding. And as far as Test cricket goes and ICC regulations say, you can't take a side off fielding. Speak to the ICC about it."'

Hussain emphasised that he had 'no problem with that', which is just as well, because otherwise umpire Venkat might have mentioned the series-clinching third Test in Karachi two years earlier, when England were chasing 176 off a minimum 44 overs in their second innings. With time running out and the ground in near-darkness, a blinking incoming batsman strode to the wicket to help Graham Thorpe steer the tourists to victory. No prizes for guessing his name.

— GASLAMP HEROES —

At least, in the account above, New Zealand could switch on some floodlights to help the cause. Back in 1889, the last match of the season at The Oval saw Surrey play Yorkshire in what became known as the Gaslamp Game. So dark was it by the end that one batsman's gloveless hands (batting gloves hadn't been invented, remember) were bleeding from the repeated impact of fast balls he couldn't see.

The idea had been sensible enough. Yorkshire had set Surrey 166 to win on the second day and, after recovering from 43–4 to 135–7, Surrey were still in with a fighting chance. Both captains agreed to carry on, believing it would save everyone the hassle of returning for a few overs on the morrow. Trouble was, with the light fading fast, Surrey's scoring rate became agonisingly slow. By now the crowd was encroaching into the outfield as they peered into the gloom.

When Sharpe was dismissed at 136, Beaumont arrived at the crease to inform the umpire, 'Bothered if I can see the ball.' Umpire Thoms replied dryly, 'If you can't see 'em, you'd best feel for 'em.' Beaumont duly did – hence his shredded hands – and with all the pavilion gaslamps ablaze saw Surrey home at 7pm (the equivalent of 8pm in today's British Summer Time).

— SPOILSPORT —

Why do some people always go and spoil things? Never in the history of Test cricket have the first four batsmen of a side each scored centuries in the same innings. Yet, on 18 June 1993, towards the end of the second day in the second Ashes Test at Lord's, the Aussie scorecard briefly read as follows:

> Mark Taylor..111
> Michael Slater 152
> David Boon..164
> Mark Waugh..99

Who spoilt the show? None other than Phil 'The Cat' Tufnell, who bowled Mark Waugh on that most agonising of scores. Waugh had to wait another eight years before posting a Lord's century, but in the context of that 1993 match, his wicket made little difference. Gooch aside, the card for England's first four didn't look terribly much like Australia's; the visitors won by an innings and 62 runs.

— DOUBLE HAT-TRICK —

It was May 1912, the memory of the *Titanic* disaster was still fresh, a UK transport strike was looming, the Home Rule Bill for Ireland was going through Parliament and militant suffragettes led by Emmeline Pankhurst were busy smashing windows in London's West End. With such a hectic news agenda, it's understandable that a Test match between two overseas sides in Manchester didn't figure prominently in the public psyche. It's a shame, however, because one of the players, Australia's little-known leg spinner Jimmy Matthews, turned in a performance never seen in a Test before or since.

The match – part of a triangular tournament between Australia, South Africa and England – saw Matthews' side take control from the outset. Responding to the Aussie's 448, the Springboks gradually clawed themselves towards the 298 needed to avoid the follow-on but were on 265–7 when Matthews was invited to turn his arm over. He promptly beat R Beaumont with a fizzer that took off-stump, trapped SJ Pegler lbw with his next ball and immediately followed this by dismissing TA Ward the same way, wrapping up the innings.

South Africa were duly sent in again and had reached a dismal 70 for 5 when, once again, Matthews got the nod from his skipper. He bowled HW Taylor almost immediately; fired out next man, RO Schwarz, with a brilliant caught-and-bowled; and discovered the new man at the crease was the hapless Ward, facing a hat-trick ball for the second time in the match.

The rest, as they say, is history. Fielders crowded around the crease, Matthews bowled, Ward prodded, the ball popped into the air, the fielding side did goldfish impressions and Matthews – deciding he couldn't leave the responsibility to anyone else – dived the full length of the pitch to take a catch inches from the ground. It was a fantastic achievement, but one on which Matthews never built; he played only eight Tests for Australia, taking just 16 wickets.

Next on the list of all-time hat-trick heroes must be Pakistan's Wasim Akram, who managed the feat twice in two weeks in the 1998/99 Asian Test Championship: first at Lahore and again in the final at Dhaka.

LAST TEN TEST HAT-TRICKS (ENGLAND)

NAME	OPPONENTS	SEASON	VENUE
M Hoggard	West Indies	2003/4	Barbados
D Gough	Australia	1998/9	Sydney
D Cork	West Indies	1995	Manchester
PJ Loader	West Indies	1957	Leeds
T Goddard	South Africa	1938/9	Johannesburg
MJ Allom	New Zealand	1929/30	Christchurch
J Hearne	Australia	1899	Leeds
G Lohmann	South Africa	1895/6	Port Elizabeth
J Briggs	Australia	1891/2	Sydney
W Bates	Australia	1882/3	Melbourne

LAST TEN TEST HAT-TRICKS (ALL COUNTRIES)

NAME	COUNTRY	OPPONENTS	SEASON	VENUE
J Franklin	New Zealand	Bangladesh	2004/5	Dhaka
M Hoggard	England	West Indies	2003/4	Barbados
A Blignaut	Zimbabwe	Bangladesh	2003/4	Harare
A Kapali	Bangladesh	Pakistan	2003	Peshawar
J Lawson	West Indies	Australia	2002/3	Bridgetown
M Sami	Pakistan	Sri Lanka	2000/1	Lahore
H Singh	India	Australia	2000/1	Kolkata
G McGrath	Australia	West Indies	2000/1	Perth
A Razzaq	Pakistan	Sri Lanka	1999/2000	Galle
N Zoysa	Sri Lanka	Zimbabwe	1999/2000	Harare
W Akram	Pakistan	Sri Lanka	1998/9	Dhaka

— SAGE SKIPPER —

Michael Vaughan's wit and wisdom since becoming England captain.

- 'You expect a bit of chin music when you come to these parts.'
  – Pre-series interview on arrival in the West Indies, 2004

- '[The Caribbean] is an incredible place and, whatever people say, it will be a fantastic venue for the World Cup. So what if a plane's a bit late and you hang around an airport for a few hours, or the PA system at the ground is up the spout?'
  – On doing a PR job for the 2007 World Cup in the West Indies

- 'The achievement that this team has achieved is a fantastic achievement.'
  – On completing a 3–0 series win in the West Indies

- 'We were in the game for about 1.2 overs.'
  – On coming second in his first ODI in Sri Lanka.
  Vaughan scored two and the hosts won by ten wickets

- 'I can party as good [*sic*] as the rest of 'em.'
  – Discussing his preferred end-of-season wind-down routine

- 'We are cramming cricket in, but there's nothing we can do about it.'
  – On England's demanding Test and ODI schedule

- 'Of course, Glenn McGrath and Shane Warne would always be in it, and so not able to take wickets.'
  – On being asked whether he favoured
  introducing a Test match sin bin

- 'Every time we snicked it, it went to hand. Every shot we played seemed to go down their throats. It was just not a good day to remember.'
  – At the end of his first disastrous day in charge as Test captain,
  when England were bowled out for 173 at Lords
  while South Africa eased to 151–1 at stumps

- 'If we had lost at Trent Bridge, I had visions of my head appearing on a turnip like [former England soccer manager] Graham Taylor on the back pages.'
  – After winning his first Test as captain against
  South Africa at Trent Bridge, 2003

- 'He's not there much at the moment. He's usually out in the middle.'
  – *On being asked to describe Andrew Flintoff's effect on the England dressing room*

— SELECTING A BATTING STROKE —

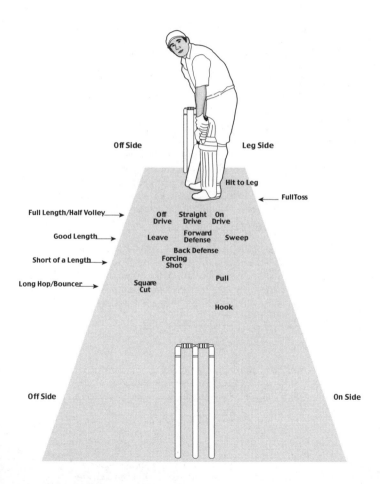

— FARE PLAY —

When the West Indies beat Australia by 17 runs in the World Cup final at Lords in 1975 (largely thanks to Clive Lloyd's 102), there was instant bedlam on the pitch as spectators celebrated. In all the chaos, poor Dickie Bird lost his distinctive white cap, which was swiped from his head as he tried to reach the pavilion.

A few days later, Bird was travelling on a double-decker across London when he noticed the West Indian conductor was wearing a familiar-looking titfer. 'Excuse me,' ventured Dickie, 'but where did you get that cap from?' Quick as a flash, the conductor replied, 'Have you heard of Dickie Bird, the Test umpire? He's my friend. He gave it to me.'

— HOW IS THAT? —

The intricacies of the lbw law rival those of soccer's offside – along with any rule you care to mention in rugby union – as the purest form of popular sporting controversy. In fact, the law itself is straightforward; the tricky bit is in applying it consistently. Here's how it works.

The principle is that an umpire will *consider* giving a batsman out lbw if he is *sure* the player's pads prevented the ball from hitting the stumps. That said, there are several cut-and-dried situations in which, even if the above is true, the batsman will be not out. Here they are:

- The ball touched the bat first;

- The ball pitched 'outside leg' – ie outside an imaginary line drawn between the batsman's leg stump and the opposite stump at the bowler's end;

- The bowler delivers a no-ball;

- The batsman is struck on the pad *outside* an imaginary line drawn between his off stump and the opposite stump at the bowler's end, *and* has made an attempt to play the ball.

For an lbw to be given, the umpire therefore must be sure that the batsman was struck pad-first in front of the stumps, and that the ball was pitched in line with the two sets of stumps.

Alternatively, the batsman may be dismissed if he is struck outside the line of off stump, provided that…

- The ball was seaming or swinging in to hit the stumps; *and*

- The batsman was making no attempt to hit the ball.

This business about what is or isn't a proper attempt to play the ball is crucial. If the rule didn't exist, batsmen could pad away every ball pitched outside off stump, causing a mass coma in the stands. However, interpretation of the rule sometimes leaves umpires completely at odds.

The best example of this came during the England–West Indies second Test at Edgbaston in 2004. As Ashley Giles was spinning the home side to victory, Shivnarine Chanderpaul adopted a canny defence by tucking his bat behind his front pad and pushing forward to everything pitched outside off stump. His aim was to convince the umpires he was playing shots, and New Zealander Simon Taufel bought the line, repeatedly turning down Giles's excitable lbw appeals.

Seeing this, an exasperated Michael Vaughan showed his nous and switched Giles to Aussie Darrell Hair's end. Vaughan knew Hair was tougher on padders and, sure enough, the first time the Chanderpaul Pad Trick was tried, up went Hair's index finger. Batsmen may complain about this naked inconsistency but if they want it expunged from the game, there's a simple solution: they can use their bats.

— IRRESISTIBLE GAME —

Cricket's greatest strength lies in its adaptability. The obvious example is Kwik Cricket – responsible for introducing thousands of young children to the game – and beach cricket, one of the few sports which whole families still play together. A lesser-known version is deck cricket, as perfected by the crew of the World War I Royal Navy battleship HMS *Irresistible*.

The crew of the *Irresistible* decided that a quick game was the perfect way to end their working day at sea and set about devising a seven-a-side format. Self-standing wickets were knocked together, chalk was used to draw a crease and the seine net was suspended around the deck to avoid the risk of 'ball overboard'. If a batsman still insisted on hitting over the top into Davy Jones's locker, his entire team was given out as a punishment.

The skill of the game therefore rested on pushing singles, and batsmen had to score off every delivery – 'tip and run', in playground parlance. This was tricky, because fielders were allowed to bowl from either end without prior warning. Batsmen became adept at the 'hatch shot', whereby the ball was chipped down a hatchway to the lower deck. This usually produced five or six runs, but even so it was rare that a side could post more than 50. Innings rarely lasted more than 15 minutes.

A modern parallel to the hatch shot came during, of all things, the very first World Cup final between West Indies and Australia at Lords in 1975. The Windies seemed to be coasting when Dennis Lillee and Jeff Thomson came together for the last wicket, still needing an unlikely 59 runs for victory. They mounted a punchy rearguard action and had reduced the run rate to 21 off two overs when Thomson hit a skier to Roy Fredricks at cover. Fredricks pouched it, but the umpire called no-ball, and Fredricks threw to the bowler's end, bringing overthrows. Meanwhile, the crowd oblivious to the no-ball signal, thought it was all over and invaded the outfield. The ball vanished in their midst and chaos reigned.

Throughout all this, a gleeful Lillee and Thomson just kept running. Eventually, umpire Tom Spencer asked them to stop, explaining that he'd called dead ball. 'How many runs did we get?' enquired a breathless Thomson? 'Two,' said Spencer. 'Take a jump in the pond,' retorted the incredulous Thommo. 'We've been running around here all afternoon and you give us two? You must be kidding.' There might have been another word between 'be' and 'kidding', but it is long lost in the mists of time. Two runs later, Thomson's wicket fell and the Windies became first ever world champions.

— CAUGHT OUT —

Like most clichés, that old dressing-room favourite 'catches win matches' is invariably true. Any doubters should cast an eye over the following table, which lists the top ten Test batsmen most frequently caught out. In most cases, half of all the dismissals are catches.

Of course, it could be argued that dropping the likes of Tendulkar hardly matters, because on the basis of these statistics he's bound to offer another chance sooner or later. Trouble is, when Sachin's in the mood, the difference between sooner and later is the difference between winning and losing.

Name	Country	Number Of Innings	Test Average	Dismissed Caught (%)
SK Warne	Australia	161	15.97	54.7
IT Botham	England	161	33.55	52.9
IA Healy	Australia	182	27.40	52.2
Inzamam-ul-Haq	Pakistan	158	49.65	52.1
AP De Silva	Sri Lanka	159	42.98	51.4
M Azharuddin	India	147	45.04	50.7
Kapil Dev	India	184	31.05	49.7
A Ranatunga	Sri Lanka	155	35.70	49.0
SR Tendulkar	India	116	56.45	47.3
DB Vengsarkar	India	185	42.13	46.0

— TOP TEN UMPIRES —

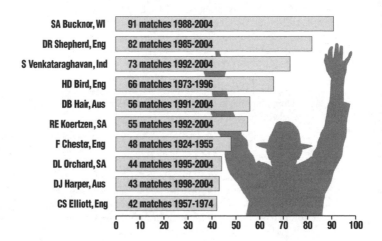

Umpire	Matches
SA Bucknor, WI	91 matches 1988-2004
DR Shepherd, Eng	82 matches 1985-2004
S Venkataraghavan, Ind	73 matches 1992-2004
HD Bird, Eng	66 matches 1973-1996
DB Hair, Aus	56 matches 1991-2004
RE Koertzen, SA	55 matches 1992-2004
F Chester, Eng	48 matches 1924-1955
DL Orchard, SA	44 matches 1995-2004
DJ Harper, Aus	43 matches 1998-2004
CS Elliott, Eng	42 matches 1957-1974

0 10 20 30 40 50 60 70 80 90 100

SPOTTERS' GUIDE TO THE TOP TEN UMPIRES

STEPHEN ANTHONY BUCKNOR

Known affectionately as 'Slow Death', on account of the agonising delay and nod that heralds the raising of his finger, Steve Bucknor is the ultimate in unflappability. An imposing 6' 3", his authority is rarely questioned, on or off the field.

DAVID ROBERT SHEPHERD

Rotund and stolid, Shepherd is the archetypal English yeoman. Raised on Devon's wild and beautiful north coast, he still helps his brother (a newsagent) with a paper round during visits home. Spectators delight in his habit of balancing on one leg whenever the score reaches a Nelson (111) or one of its multiples.

SRINIVAS VENKATARAGHAVAN

Indian umpires are rarities on the international circuit, but Venkat is rightly revered as a master of the art. Cheerful and disarming, his unusual claim to fame is that his best bowling figures in a 19-year Test career came in his very first series, against New Zealand, when he took 8–72.

HAROLD DENNIS BIRD
Flat white cap, diminutive, slightly round-shouldered (all those years spent crouching over stumps), even in retirement 'Dickie' is one of the best-loved figures in the game. His tactic for dissuading fire-breathing fast bowlers from over-sledging went something like, 'Now, now. You know you don't really mean all those nasty things you're saying.'

DARRELL BRUCE HAIR
Hair is easily distinguishable by his bulk and cry of 'NA-BAWL' when Muttiah Muralitharan is bowling. His concern about Murali's action (he actually described it as 'diabolical' in his autobiography) caused a huge ruckus among the Asian Test nations.

RUDOLF ERIC KOERTZEN
The Arnie Schwarzenegger of the Test circuit, Koertzen is something of a gym junkie, whose trademark accessory at the crease is a pair of rather sinister wraparound sunglasses. Before Tests, he relaxes by studying video footage of the players' previous dismissals. Talk about Total Recall.

FRANK CHESTER
Chester could be tetchy during matches, especially if his stomach ulcers were giving him gyp. He was the first of the real 'low stoopers', believing it made lbw decisions more reliable, and his verdicts were always prompt. He died in 1957, two years after his retirement.

DAVID LYNTON ORCHARD
Another member of the portly club, Orchard's understated white beard and abrupt manner give him an aura of wisdom. Some would argue that the aura doesn't always work, like when he failed to give a glaring run-out against Graham Thorpe in the first Test of the 1995/6 South Africa versus England series.

DARYL JOHN HARPER
Balding and with a ready grin, Harper has taken more than his fair share of (unwarranted) criticism for bias, supposedly against Sri Lanka. He has a reputation for shrugging off stick from the media.

CHARLES STANDISH ELLIOTT
A highly respected figure, Charlie Elliott combined a successful county cricket career at Derbyshire before World War II with a professional contract at Coventry City FC. He stood in 42 Tests in the days before neutral umpires were the norm.

— BOTTY DAZZLER —

Maybe it's his rich Yorkshire accent, his fine pair of shoulders or that cheeky-chappie grin. Whatever, Darren 'Dazzler' Gough is regarded as top cricket totty by women in India and his appearances as a Sky TV pundit during the 2003 World Cup in South Africa set hearts a-fluttering across the subcontinent.

'The mail I got from India was absolutely unbelievable,' Dazzler told the *Sunday Times*. 'Love letters. Flowers were being sent to South Africa from India with little notes from women. I only worked on telly there for a week, but I got a great response. I think it was my voice that did it – like Geoff Boycott's. He was popular in India, too.'

While the thought of Boycott as a pin-up icon is slightly discomfiting, it's as nothing to the career change planned for Gough by the celebrated Bollywood producer Bobby Khan. Khan met Darren after the World Cup to offer him a role in an English-speaking film alongside a well-known UK model. 'Trouble is,' says Dazzler, 'they want me to be filmed walking away from the camera naked, so you'd see my bottom from behind. I'd have to get proper fitness training then. You wouldn't get me out of the gym for a month.'

It's true that the Gough buttocks would, to put it delicately, frighten the horses. Even so, they must be in better shape than his knees. Like most quick bowlers, Gough's delivery stride transfers seven times his body weight through the leading leg – effectively a 700kg hammer-blow which literally chips away at knee cartilage. To repair some of the damage, he has been under the care of German homeopathic specialist Dr Hans Muller-Wolfhart, a man who handles some of the most famous joints in sport. Part of the medicinal cocktail injected by Dr Hans into Darren's knees is taken from a cock's comb, the erect quiff on top of a young cock's head. That should be an interesting conversational opener for any Indian lady lucky enough to get close to Dazzler. Let's hope nothing gets lost in translation.

— SOBERING THOUGHT —

Considering that he's the greatest Test all-rounder ever, with 8,032 runs at an average 57.78 and 235 wickets at 34, Sir Garry Sobers' ODI figures make depressing reading. They go something like this: 'Played one, lost one, scored nought. Bowling average: 31.' His one consolation is that he castled Chris Old – the England paceman who had earlier dismissed him for a duck – in the 1973 Prudential Trophy match at Headingley. By then, he was 37 years old and past his best.

Far better to remember Sir Garry for that glorious day – 31 August 1968 – at St Helens, Swansea, when, during an innings for Nottinghamshire, he struck Glamorgan's unfortunate Malcolm Nash for six consecutive sixes. Nash saw his first two balls carted into the stand next to the Cricketer's Inn. The third landed in the pavilion enclosure and the fourth disappeared over the scoreboard.

There was a brief ray of hope when the fifth ball was driven straight to fielder Roger Davis, who caught it. Unfortunately, he then fell over the rope, turning poor Nash's prized scalp into yet another six.

Just before the final delivery, wicket-keeper Eifion Jones mischievously bet Sobers he couldn't hit six from six. The great man grinned, lifted his bat and deposited the ball out of the ground. Sporting legends don't come bigger.

It seems ludicrous that, after the end of his first-class career, the West Indies Cricket Board waited 30 years to give Sobers a meaningful coaching role in their international squad. In the wake of the Windies' 2004 ICC Champions' Trophy victory, he was finally named as technical consultant to work alongside former Australian National Academy director Bennett King. But maybe it's unfair to criticise the WICB for failing to utilise a true cricket genius, and maybe they did try hard over the years to get him on board. Maybe.

Incidentally, Sobers' bat that day in Swansea was a short-handle Slazenger (although, with the mood he was in, you could have chucked him a broom handle and he'd have clouted bowlers into oblivion). It was sold by auction house Christie's at Melbourne in 2000 for £54,257, comfortably exceeding the £47,476 paid for the bat he used to establish a then world record 365 runs against Pakistan in Kingston in 1958.

If you're reading this, Sir Garry, and you've got any tatty old bats cluttering up the place, do let us know. We'll pay the postage.

— JOB LOT —

In common with those of most other professional sports, cricket careers are getting shorter. More matches, tougher physical demands and an increasing pool of young talent means that older Test stars simply cannot play the reputation card to hold their place. To illustrate this, we've compared two England sides that played in an Ashes Christmas Test at Melbourne: one in 1950, the other in 1990. The tables show the length of each player's Test career and the age at which he eventually quit Test cricket or was dropped. As you'll see, the average career of the 1990s player was approximately three years and 22 weeks shorter than his counterpart of the 1950s. His time as a candidate for top level cricket is also less – around 11 years on average, as opposed to 16.

For the 1950 side, we've cheated slightly by deselecting opener Reg Simpson and number three John Dewes and replacing them with Denis Compton and Bill Edrich. Dewes' Test career lasted just three years, never giving him a chance to fulfil his huge potential, while opener Simpson was rarely an automatic choice. Compton, on the other hand, would have been first on the team sheet if he hadn't been injured, and the exclusion of Edrich from that particular tour party was rightly greeted with disbelief among the cricketing public. As for Brian Close getting a Test recall at 45, that's admittedly bizarre, but he skews the comparison only slightly.

MCC 1950 (VERSUS AUSTRALIA, SECOND TEST)

NAME	TEST CAREER	TOTAL TEST YEARS	AGE AT LAST TEST
Bill Edrich	1938–55	17	38
Cyril Washbrook	1937–56	19	41
Denis Compton	1937–57	20	38
Len Hutton	1937–55	18	38
Gilbert Parkhouse	1950–9	9	33
Brian Close	1949–76	27	45
Freddie Brown	1931–53	22	42
Trevor Bailey	1949–59	10	35
Godfrey Evans	1946–59	13	38
Alec Bedser	1946–55	9	37
Doug Wright	1938–51	13	36

TEAM AVERAGES
Test years – 16 years, four weeks
Age at last test – 38 years, ten weeks

MCC 1990 (VERSUS AUSTRALIA, SECOND TEST)

NAME	TEST CAREER	TOTAL TEST YEARS	AGE AT LAST TEST
Graham Gooch	1975-1995	20	41
Michael Atherton	1989-2001	12	33
Wayne Larkins	1979-91	12	37
Robin Smith	1988-96	8	32
David Gower	1978-92	14	35
Alec Stewart	1989-2003	14	40
Jack Russell	1988-98	10	34
Phil DeFreitas	1986-95	9	29
Angus Fraser	1989-99	10	33
Devon Malcolm	1989-97	8	34
Phil Tufnell	1990-2001	11	35

TEAM AVERAGES
Test years: 11 years, 30 weeks
Age at last test: 34 years, 40 weeks

As time at the top shortens, so today's cricketers are adapting to a mid-30s career shift. Here's what some of the current multi-skilled generation are up to:

NAME	COUNTY	OTHER LIFE
Martyn Ball	Gloucestershire	Insurance
Peter Bowler	Somerset	Solicitor
Martin Bicknell	Surrey	Golf-equipment website
Darren Bicknell	Nottinghamshire	Advertising
Dougie Brown	Warwickshire	Spanish-property agent
Kevin Dean	Derbyshire	Bookmaker chain
Jason Gallian	Nottinghamshire	Sports media training
Paul Grayson	Essex	Essex Academy coach
Ben Hutton	Middlesex	City insurer
David Leatherdale	Worcestershire	Marketing
Richard Montgomerie	Sussex	Marketing
Graham Napier	Essex	Website design
Paul Nixon	Leicestershire	Spanish-property agent
James Pipe	Worcestershire	Physiotherapy
Andy Pratt	Durham	Plumber
Martin Saggers	Kent	Wildlife photographer
Billy Taylor	Hampshire	Tree surgeon
Mark Turner	Durham	Retail display adviser
Rob Turner	Somerset	Stockbroker
Rob White	Northamptonshire	Accountant
Matt Windows	Gloucestershire	Accountant

— YANKED SHOULDERS —

It comes to something when Englishmen need an American to teach them to play cricket properly, but hey, at least it shows they're interested in proper sport over there. England's fielding 'tsar', Mike Young, is a former Major League baseball coach who worked with both the Cleveland Indians and the Baltimore Orioles. He also did a stint with the Australian Test side after telling the management he knew nothing about cricket and would take nothing for granted. And you thought *everyone* lied on job application forms.

From the moment Young joined the ECB Academy for a month-long stint, in October 2004, he began questioning decades of received fielding wisdom. Test players, he said, risked serious injury because they'd never been shown how to throw correctly. Sliding stops were also flawed – QED fast bowler Simon Jones's horrific rupture of a cruciate ligament while trying to prevent a four on the first morning of the 2002/3 Ashes series. At the time, MCC management blamed the Gabba's rough, sandy outfield; Young insists that Jones's 'technique on the slide was terrible'.

In an interview with *The Sun*, he went on: 'It can make so much difference to the outcome of a match to get the small things right. If we don't focus on fielding, we're going to keep getting people hurt. We've got a lot of shoulder injuries because players at the highest level are not practising throwing enough.'

His toughest words, though, are reserved for that shibboleth of cricket masters and youth coaches across the nation: the need for players to 'walk in' with the bowler. This is supposedly to get fielders moving and ready for action. Rubbish, says Young. 'I've seen some guys take 14 steps in, then, after the ball's bowled, they take 14 steps back again. Fourteen steps! There and back, every ball, for three hours. That's three kilometres! No wonder a guy's a bit tired. I ask players why they do it, I get a variety of answers, like "That's the way I was taught" or "To keep awake." It doesn't make any sense.'

Young suggests that, as a bowler hits delivery stride, fielders instead adopt the 'split step', a balanced stance similar to that of a tennis player receiving serve. He urges sides to field 'like a pack of wolves', with at least two chasing every shot, and to throw low for run-outs. Most importantly, he likes coaches to keep a tally of runs saved during games.

The one Young innovation that still needs honing, however, is his method of stopping 'fog out' – a lack of concentration – among fielders. In Australia, he persuaded the bowlers to send secret signals indicating that the next delivery would be different – perhaps a bouncer or maybe a disguised slower ball. 'It was interesting for a few overs,' he says ruefully, 'but then the fielders forgot to watch for them.'

— AGIN GANGULY —

Indian captain Sourav Ganguly's tactic of slowing over rates has given him a nasty shock. His chin-wagging with bowlers and juggling of fielding positions is well known in the Test arena, where batsmen face the serious prospect of being bored out. However, following Indian cricket's 75th anniversary showpiece against Pakistan in November 2004 he was blamed for delaying the finish by over an hour. A hearing in front of match referee Clive Lloyd went against him and he was hit with a two-match suspension.

According to Clause C1 of the ICC Code of Conduct, a fielding side should take an average 4 minutes 12 seconds to get through an over during a 50 overs-per-side one-dayer. That's one ball every 42 seconds – a reasonable target, as long as fielders aren't getting over a heavy night in the bar. On average, Ganguly took roughly half a minute longer per over, and although failure to meet the rate wouldn't normally carry a suspension, the Indian skipper had 'previous' from an identical recent transgression.

Ultimately, the suspension was lifted by Tim Castle, the ICC Appeals Commissioner, after he accepted that the delays were not all Ganguly's fault. There were frequent interruptions in the game (which Pakistan won by six wickets), including *eight* ball changes and various injuries. Time will tell whether Ganguly has finally got the message.

— THE MYSTERIOUS AFFAIR AT TORRE —

It was a case to stump the Queen of Crime herself, a bizarre whodunnit set around the historic cricket club faithfully supported by Agatha Christie.

In the summer of 2004, senior members of Torquay CC – of whom Christie's father, Frederick Alvah Miller, was once president – became convinced that a piqued insider motivated by revenge was behind attempts to sabotage their season. The crucial clue was a rather unChristie-like incoming call number retrieved from a mobile-phone SIM card.

The first attack, at the beginning of May 2004, occurred after dark at the club's sea-front Recreation Ground, sandwiched between the Grand Hotel – where Christie spent her honeymoon – and Torre Abbey, home of the exhibition that celebrates her Torquay upbringing. On this occasion, groundsmen's hoses were dragged from the boundary, poked under the covers and turned on. The resulting flood threatened the first XI's opening game in the Francis Clark Devon League Premier Division, and only a huge mopping-up exercise saved the day.

Then, in June, a man claiming to represent Torquay thirds rang league rivals Exeter St James to call off a fixture at short notice. He said that Torquay were unable to raise a side, although this was news to the 11 cricketers who, an hour later, arrived in Exeter ready to play. By then the home side had disappeared, stood down by their captain, Ryan Keary. The visitors were left to scratch their heads and contemplate a 12-point deduction by the Partnership Publishing South Devon Cricket League for defaulting on the game.

Mr Keary said that the cancellation call had been made to a previous Exeter St James captain, who, though puzzled, accepted it in good faith and passed the message on. 'Fortunately, his phone retained the hoaxer's number,' said Mr Keary. 'The Torquay players accused me of making the call, claiming I'd struggled to get a side. That was total rubbish. I had the pick of 20 players and was very confident of winning.'

Torquay's chairman, solicitor Stephen Craig, later told newspapers that the hose and hoax incidents were almost certainly the work of a single player with a grudge. 'Everyone has their suspicions,' he said. 'I completed my inquiries and the committee gave one particular gentleman seven days to resign. Cricket is supposed to be a gentlemen's game, played by gentlemen, but this individual has acted in a truly malicious, vindictive way. Every club in the country could be affected by people like this. It amounts to absolute anarchy.'

Founded in 1851, Torquay CC is among the oldest clubs in the country. Christie's American father was the club's president during the 1890s and passed his love of the summer game on to his daughter. By the time she published her first novel – *The Mysterious Affair At Styles*, featuring Hercule Poirot – in 1920, she was a regular spectator at Torquay's ground. The author's grandson, Mathew Prichard, said, 'My grandmother loved cricket and would come and watch me playing at school whenever she could, but I've no idea what she would make of this sabotage business. It does rather sound like a case for Poirot or Miss Marple.'

— LIKE RABBITS —

Nasser Hussain has revealed that his family called him Bunny because he ate a lot of carrots. That must be the right reason because, leaving aside the other thing those floppy-eared vermin are famous for, his batting could never be said to be rabbit-like. In 96 Tests, Hussain posted 14 centuries and 33 half-centuries.

The King of the Bunnies in international cricket is, of course, Courtney Walsh, who managed no fewer than 54 ducks in his 337 matches. That doesn't seem too bad until you count up all the DNBs (Did Not Bat) against his name. For most of his career, opposing bowlers could only dream of getting far enough down the formidable West Indies batting line-up to have a pop at Courtney.

Here's a list of the top five bunny greats for both Tests and ODIs. At the time of writing, it's worth pointing out that Muralitharan and Warne are not only battling for the title of all-time leading wicket-taker; they're also edging their way to Walsh's fur-lined crown.

NAME	NUMBER OF DUCKS
Courtney Walsh	54
Wasim Akram	45
Muttiah Muralitharan	42
Shane Warne	40
Curtley Ambrose	39

— CUTTING A DASH WITH A 'TACHE —

The Adolf

The Fine Cut

The Terry-Thomas

The Lord Lucan

The Mexican

The Merve The Swerve

THE ADOLF	
Description	Had a bad press over the years. Wearers like to dictate the game.
Advantage	Neat and unfussy. Little dressing-room grooming required.
Disadvantage	Easy for team-mates to mock by placing two fingers horizontally beneath nose.
Best Exponent	Former Aussie skipper-turned-commentator Ian Chappell.

THE FINE CUT

Description	Appears to have been drawn on as a joke.
Advantage	Opponents get distracted while trying to spot if it's really there.
Disadvantage	Batsmen snick it too easily while shaving, adding to general ridicule.
Best Exponents	Windies skipper Brian Lara; Zimbabwe's Tatenda Taibu.

THE TERRY-THOMAS

Description	Conjures up memories of warm beer, summer afternoon cricket, elderly ladies cycling around the village green and whatever else was in that John Major speech aimed at getting voters to elect him, which they didn't.
Advantage	Can be waxed up between overs to confuse batsmen.
Disadvantage	Won't fit inside a helmet.
Best Exponent	19th century Australian legend Fred Spofforth.

THE LORD LUCAN

Description	Lush, black and curving, the Lucan can give its wearer either a supercilious or a deadpan image.
Advantage	Provides an air of unfluffability, offering psychological edge out in the middle. Also, no worries about waiting for growth; any good make-up-and-disguise kit will include a stick-on one.
Disadvantage	Opposing supporters shout taunts such as 'Haven't I seen you riding Shergar?'
Best Exponents	Former England opener Graham Gooch; Aussie power-merchant David 'Stumpy' Boon.

THE MEXICAN

Description	Well, Mexican.
Advantage	Very, very menacing.
Disadvantage	Easily lost in stubble on no-shave days when reporting late to pavilion.
Best Exponents	Aussie demon Dennis Lillee; England 'keeper-turned-artist Jack Russell.

The Merv The Swerve

Description	The ultimate in cricketing facial chic.
Advantage	Sponsors die for distinctive lip-wear like this.
Disadvantage	Bits of breakfast dislodged in delivery stride may strike umpire between eyes. Marginal lbw decisions may consequently go in batsmen's favour.

Best (and only) Exponent: Merv Hughes.

— PASTA JOKE —

As every student knows, flatmates sometimes push you close to the edge. Especially when they let slip some little fact about your personal life that, actually, you'd rather the world didn't know. It's obviously worse if you're the rising star of Australian Test cricket and your youthful foible is revealed to the dressing room. Let's face it, there might be teasing.

Imagine, then, how Australian pin-up Michael Clarke – nicknamed 'Pup' by his team-mates – must have felt on reading a press interview with his old mucker Ayick Gene, a former international soccer player and captain of Sydney United who shacked up with Clarke at the request of the batsman's manager, Neil D'Costa. Despite a 15-year age gap, D'Costa believed his young charge could benefit from the experience of a hardened professional sportsman. It seems he was right: Pup bashed 376 runs in his first three Tests against India, and although he managed only 24 in the fourth (when Australia were skittled for 93 in their second innings), his slow left-arm spin produced 6 for 9 in 6.2 overs.

Gene's recollections start innocuously enough. 'He's a young, cocky guy and he's pretty sure of himself,' he says, 'but at the same time he's very respectful of his seniors, and loyal.' Then comes the (kitchen) knife in the back: 'I'd come home and he'd always be cooking pasta, then washing all the dishes.'

So, now we know: the darling of Australia's middle order is a spag-bol merchant who wallows in domestic servitude and nurses an acute case of dishpan hands. If you were Michael Clarke, you'd surely be thinking, 'Thanks for that, Ayick.' Still, at least it clears up the 'Pup' moniker, which is nothing to do with young dogs or pin-ups; it's short for 'pasta's up'.

— BALLS TO NEIGHBOURS —

Bearing in mind that Australia is a sport-loving, sport-*winning* nation, this next item really is baffling. The state of Victoria has changed the laws of cricket so that batsmen who hit a six get officially warned by the umpires and told that it doesn't count. If a player hits another, five runs are deducted from his team's score. Really. In theory, all 10,000 cricket clubs across the country could be affected.

At the time of writing, the battle is centred on 100 Eastern Cricket Associations, mostly those in close proximity to houses. There have been complaints from residents about the risk of injury or damage caused by flying balls but, unsurprisingly, that view doesn't wash with club regulars like bowler Henry Gregory, of Canterbury, who told his local paper that the whingers should stay inside or wear helmets, a suggestion that could make a great subplot for *Neighbours*; it's hard to see though how you can swig a tinnie over the barbie when your titfer is a Masuri titanium Full Face.

Anyway, Henry was clearly in no mood for compromise. 'During one game, the ball simply landed in some woman's front yard and she was straight out of the door and moaning,' he said. 'We're not yobs purposely trying to annoy the neighbours. Some of the complaints really do stem from a bunch of moaning minnies.' Second XI skipper Glenn Sanguinetti agreed: 'Aussies have always been known for being aggressive batsmen. We like to feel the strike of leather on the bat. That's what Australian cricket is all about. We want to get value for a shot and be rewarded with runs for a good hit. Now it means that we have to modify our game to please the neighbours.'

Perhaps, the threat of adding minus five to the scoreboard isn't such a bad thing. It brings to mind the story of Aussie left-hander Neil Harvey, who, on a 1948 Ashes tour to England, wanted some batting tips from the top. He asked his team-mate Sam Loxton to approach captain Don Bradman for suggestions. 'Tell Loxton to keep the ball on the ground,' advised The Don. 'Then he won't get caught.'

— RULED OUT —

Most rules in cricket are fairly clear-cut. The problem is remembering them in the heat of the moment. Here are five classic howlers to avoid at all costs.

THE DOLLY DILLY DALLY

Former England all-rounder Basil D'Oliveira was making his debut for England at Lord's in June 1966 against a handy-looking West Indies side. His innings didn't start too well (he was dropped off the second ball) but recovered his nerves and had made 27 when a hard drive from Jim Parks hit him at the non-striker's end and deflected onto the stumps, dislodging the bails.

Basil, who had been backing up, stood out of his crease, wondering if he was out. He wasn't – at least not yet, because the ball needed to have touched a fielder first. Unfortunately Dolly dallied too long, Wes Hall picked up a stump, held it against the ball and successfully appealed for a run out. 'Sorry, Bas,' said Wes.

THE PROCTOR SHOCKER

South African all-round supremo Mike Proctor was playing for Natal against Transvaal in the 1967/8 season when he was called upon to bowl a tense final ball. Transvaal had been in charge throughout and needed just 58 for victory in their second innings. Alas, with the scores level, there was a huge cloudburst.

The umpires realised that, once the teams went off, the game would never restart. They decided to allow one more ball, which meant that, provided Natal could stop a run, they would achieve an improbable tie. Aware that a leg bye would be enough, stand-in skipper Barry Versfield moved another fielder behind square leg. Unfortunately, neither he nor his bowler heard Lee Irvine shouting from the long-leg boundary. Proctor bowled, batsman Eddie Barlow swung, the stumps clattered, but the Natal celebrations were peremptory. That extra fielder was one too many on the leg side. The no-ball provided Transvaal's winning run.

THE WHADDYASAY?

Communication is everything in cricket, so when Australia found their promising start to the first Ashes Test, at Nottingham in 1953, going pear-shaped, skipper Lindsay Hassett made sure his next batsman, wicket-keeper Don Tallon, knew the strategy was to play for time. 'Give the light a go when you get in, Don,' said Hassett. Soon afterwards, another wicket fell, reducing the Aussies to 81 for 6. Knowing Tallon was a trifle deaf, Hassett repeated the order as his 'keeper strode from the changing room: 'Don't forget to give it a go.'

Over the next few overs, Hassett looked on in disbelief as his batsmen launched a flurry of clubbing blows against the equally disbelieving England bowlers. Tallon was caught for 15 trying to thump the ball into oblivion and arrived back at the dressing room in apologetic mood. 'Sorry, skip,' he said. 'We tried to give it a go, but the light was bloody terrible.'

Australia got away with it...but only just. Chasing a target of 229, England ran out of time on 120–1, with Hutton and Simpson undefeated and the likes of Compton, Graveney, May and Bailey still to come.

THE RUNNER DEAN
In the first England vs Australia ODI at Old Trafford in 1989, Aussie batsman Dean Jones was sent out as a runner for Ian Healy, who was struggling with a dodgy knee. (The Laws permit this where a batsman is genuinely injured, and the tourists' skipper, Alan Border, didn't want his 'keeper crocked ahead of the first Test.) Unfortunately, in the heat of battle, Healy couldn't stop himself dashing for a run with Jones. England skipper David Gower immediately questioned the severity of the injury and the umpires duly sent Jones back to the pavilion. Healy got to ten before he was caught by John Emburey off Neil Foster and sidled off for the hairdryer treatment from skipper Alan Border.

THE REAL CORKER
England all-rounder Dominic Cork must have known the gods were smiling on him during the 1995 fourth Test against the West Indies at Old Trafford. He took 4–45 in the first innings, followed this up with an undefeated maiden half-century and then bagged Richardson, Murray and Hooper for England's first Test hat-trick since 1957.

In fact, Cork's half-century should never have happened. He dislodged a bail while playing his first scoring shot of the day (an all-run four), but the West Indians fielders didn't spot it and didn't bother with an appeal. Umpire Cyril Mitchley wordlessly replaced the bail, England won the match by six wickets and went on to draw the series.

— CATCHES LOSE CHAMPIONSHIPS —

Bowlers have long memories, especially when it comes to dropped catches. But the spat that erupted between former Sussex captain Robin Marlar (a 'gentleman') and his one-time wicket-keeper Rupert Webb (a 'player') wouldn't have been out of place in an episode of *Dr Who*.

In an article for the cricketing bible *Wisden* on Sussex's 2003 county championship win (the first in its 165-year history), Mr Marlar suggested that the title could and should have come a lot earlier. 'I was personally convinced we were going to win in 1953,' he wrote, '…until Rupert Webb missed a vital catch behind the stumps at Hastings against Yorkshire.' He went on: 'There may be an element of bias here since I was bowling at the time and had turned an off-break away from the left-hander, Vic Wilson.'

That comment meant the gloves were off, as far as Mr Webb was concerned. 'I was a bit upset,' he told the *Daily Telegraph*. 'Just as one swallow doesn't make a summer, so one catch doesn't lose a championship, and now it has been in *Wisden* everyone in cricket will believe it to be true. I am sure he dropped some catches that year, too, and I checked his records for bowling in the seven games after the Yorkshire match. He took 11 wickets for 667 runs. That's abysmal.' The Yorkshire game proved to be the turning point of Sussex's 1953 season; afterwards, they drew every match to let arch-rivals Surrey clinch top spot.

Mr Webb said he'd approached team-mates about the day in question – 24 July – and none of them could remember his alleged blunder. Even Rob Boddie, the Sussex county cricket librarian, was dubious. 'There is no record of a dropped catch in the game,' said Mr Boddie. 'In fact, in the first innings Rupert caught Vic Wilson off Robin's bowling. But I've studied the scorebook, and it would be very surprising if George Washer, the scorer, hadn't followed his normal practice of writing a note to record a dropped catch. There's nothing.'

In his *Wisden* piece, Mr Marlar, Sussex captain between 1955 and 1959 and cricket correspondent of the *Sunday Times* for 26 years until 1996, noted that Mr Webb became an actor after retiring from cricket. He played the father of Hugh Grant's bride in *Four Weddings And A Funeral*, 'which some might think constitutes greater glory than any championship.'

After hearing of his former 'keeper's chagrin, Mr Marlar was only slightly conciliatory. 'Rupert is a fine fellow and was a very amiable colleague,' he said. 'I'm sorry he is upset, but the facts are the facts. Championships do turn on one incident. It has always happened in cricket, and it still does.'

— STAGE FRIGHT —

What do you suppose makes Andrew Strauss nervous? A Test match debut as England opener in front of a full house at Lord's, perhaps? No. If you recall, he smiled his way through a TV interview, then strode to the middle to score 112 off New Zealand.

What about facing a formidable Aussie pace attack in the ICC Champions' Trophy semi-final, then? Not really. 'If you let the ball travel almost past you before you hit it, you can achieve some great angles' was his post-match response after an undefeated 52. (By the way, Andrew, we non-batsmen really *hate* comments like that. Just a thought.)

In fact, what gets the Strauss nerves juddering is the sight of his Australian actress wife, Ruth, stepping on stage for an opening night. Perhaps it's because he feels part of the show. He certainly got his name in the credits for painting the set and managing props at one of her recent appearances in the musical *Long Gone Lonesome Cowgirls*, set in 1960s Queensland and staged at Islington's Old Red Lion Theatre. 'I mostly painted blue sky,' he says, modestly.

— ZERO TOLERANCE —

Take a look at the following international XI, ranked according to the number of Test innings they played. All are top-drawer batsmen, all have had long and distinguished careers and most have achieved a highly respectable average of 40 or more. There's one other cricketing distinction that unites them, however, and to any young player nervous about representing school, club or county for the first time, this list should be lasered into the memory.

NAME	COUNTRY	NUMBER OF INNINGS	TEST AVERAGE
GA Gooch	England	215	42.58
MA Atherton	England	212	37.70
GR Viswanath	India	155	41.93
RB Richardson	West Indies	146	44.40
L Hutton	England	138	56.67
MS Atapattu	Sri Lanka	137	39.62
KF Barrington	England	131	58.67
HP Tillakaratne	Sri Lanka	131	42.88
KWR Fletcher	England	96	39.90
HA Gomes	West Indies	91	39.64
Saeed Anwar	Pakistan	91	45.53

You will by now have spotted the connection: all of the above scored a duck on their international Test debut. For some, the baptism was both painful and sadistically lengthy; poor old Marvan Atapattu, for instance, troubled the scorers as follows in his first three Tests: 0, 0, 1, 0, 0 and 0. To really beat himself up, he also went for nought in his first ODI.

In the team above, Atapattu has the most number of ducks to his name (21), followed by Atherton (20), Gooch (13), Viswanath (10), Tillakaratne (9), Anwar and Richardson (both 8), Fletcher (6) and Barrington, Hutton and Gomes (all 5). In defence of these players, it should be pointed out that they batted against the best bowlers and, often, a new ball. In a combined total of 1,543 innings, 110 zeros works out at average 'duck rate' of just 7.12%.

Contrast that with the entertaining performances of some celebrated tail enders. Here's the all-time top ten* of Test cricket's greatest duckmen, complete

* As at 2004

with their percentage of big, fat zeros. Courtney is in a class of his own in terms of the number of dismissals, but team-mate Merv Dillon has by far the worst overall record – out for nought every third visit to the crease! (In case you hadn't noticed, Atapattu has crept in there at number ten. He's not being picked on. Honest!)

NAME	COUNTRY	INNINGS	NUMBER OF DUCKS	DUCK RATE (%)
CA Walsh	West Indies	185	43	23.2
SK Warne	Australia	161	30	18.6
GD McGrath	Australia	113	28	24.7
CE Ambrose	West Indies	145	26	17.9
MV Dillon	West Indies	68	26	38.2
M Muralitharan	Sri Lanka	117	25	21.3
DK Morrison	New Zealand	71	24	33.8
BS Chandrasekhar	India	80	23	28.7
SR Waugh	Australia	260	22	8.4
MS Atapattu	Sri Lanka	137	21	15.3

Until 2004, Courtney Walsh held the record – together with Pakistan's Wasim Akram – for inflicting the largest number of Test ducks (79 apiece). Australia's Glenn McGrath has since moved ahead of them, and duck trivia specialists (yes, you know you're out there) wait with mounting tension to see if he will end his career having inflicted precisely three times as many ducks with the ball as he registered with the bat. By the end of the 2004 India–Australia series, this ratio stood at 2.73, recurring. The tension is all too much.

— THE LATE DEVELOPER —

It's never too late for a call-up. In 1950, Raja Maharaj Singh became the oldest man ever to make his debut in first-class cricket when he played in the Bombay Governor's XI against Frank Worrell's Commonwealth XI at Bombay. He made four, wasn't asked to bowl and took no catches. He didn't grace the first-class game again, but, at the age of 72, you can see why.

— 'SCHELLE OUT —

As if there aren't enough problems out in the middle. Now the Delhi Police vice squad has come up with another that could leave many Test stars – and all club cricketers – guilty as charged. The crime is batting recklessly, and the current suspect-in-chief is none other than South Africa's Herschelle Gibbs, who was allegedly approached by the late, disgraced Hansie Cronje to help fix matches. So concerned was Gibbs at the prospect of having his collar felt that he pulled out of the Proteas winter 2004 tour to India.

The background to the Cronje match-fixing scandal is long and complex – two characteristics that make it a no-no for these hallowed pages. Suffice it to say that in 2000 the Delhi Plods tape-recorded some of Cronje's phone conversations, proving that he'd taken bungs from Indian bookmakers. Gibbs had allegedly been approached by his skipper to get out for a low score in a one-day game. He later served a six-month suspension for his part in the whole shabby affair.

Four years later, Delhi police chief KK Paul made it clear that he wasn't going to let the matter lie. He wanted to know why Gibbs 'batted recklessly' in an ODI against India in 2000, and faxed a long list of questions to the South African's lawyer, Peter Whelan. Whelan, unhappy at the cut of Paul's jib, advised his client to steer well clear of the subcontinent for a while.

For readers baffled by the mechanics of cricket betting – particularly spread betting – here's why it can be *so* profitable for a Test player to take the bookie's shilling. Let's say you fancy a flutter on England's total runs in their first innings against South Africa. Your bookmaker quotes 300–320, which means that, if you 'buy' England runs, you're backing the team to score more than 320. Conversely, if you 'sell', you're hoping that the Proteas knock them over for fewer than 300.

Suppose you buy at £1 a run. Michael Vaughan and Freddie Flintoff tank the bowling and England amass a first-innings total of 480. Pass the Bollinger – you're £160 up. However if Pollock & Co. skittle England for a humiliating 130, you've finished 170 short of the spread and therefore *owe* your bookmaker £170. The more you stake per run – or 'point' in spread-betting parlance – the more you stand to win or lose. As a safeguard, you can set a 'stop-loss' instruction to ensure that the bet automatically closes when losses hit a certain point.

Of course, many punters prefer to bet on individuals rather than teams, and this is where a bent batsman can make serious money. An in-form player quoted at 45–65 might not be too upset at getting out recklessly for 15 if he knows his bookie partner has just sold runs at £200, ensuring a net profit of £6,000. That's just one example. In any single game there are dozens of different bets and combinations that *could* be fixed, and there are plenty of shadowy types around the world to do the fixing.

The problem in all this is to decide what 'batting recklessly' actually means. Have you taken a bung if you attack from the start or from an apparently hopeless position? If so, Adam Gilchrist, you're nicked, son. Does it mean a batsman mustn't attempt risky shots even when he can play them effortlessly in his sleep? Sachin Tendulkar, you're toast. And what about pulling the world's quickest bowlers from outside off stump? Sir Viv Richards, Ian Botham – how *could* you?

Match-fixing is a cancer. Bent players should be kicked out. But reckless? Cricket needs a bit of reckless.

— VIVACIOUS VIV —

The fastest century in Test cricket was scored by the incomparable Sir Vivian Richards, who managed it on 15 April 1986, the fourth day of the fifth Test at St John's, Antigua. Richards hit 100 in 56 balls, and by the time he'd finished the England team must have been desperate to sneak off early to the airport. In fairness, they did wait one more day to be beaten (by 240 runs) and blackwashed (5–0).

Some batsmen seem to prefer a five-day booking on full board, and here's a list of the only players to have batted on every day of a five-day Test match.

Name	Team	First/Second Innings	Opponents	Venue	Season
M Jaisimha	India	20/74	Australia	Calcutta	1959/60
G Boycott	England	107/80	Australia	Nottingham	1977
K Hughes	Australia	117/84	England	Lord's	1980
A Lamb	England	23/110	West Indies	Lord's	1984
R Shastri	India	111/7	England	Calcutta	1984/5

— STICKY WICKETS —

At the end of the 19th century, a promising young left-arm spinner was casting around for a county prepared to put him on the payroll. He got a trial with Warwickshire, only to be told, 'Thanks, but no thanks.' Big, big mistake.

The young man was Wilfred Rhodes, and for the next three decades he regularly and ruthlessly reminded Warwickshire's coaching staff of just how badly they had messed up. In a 30-year career, Rhodes took 4,184 first-class wickets (still a record, by a country mile), scored 39,802 runs (including 58 centuries) and pouched 708 catches. He spent almost his entire career with Yorkshire, helping them to 11 county championships at a time when Warwickshire managed just the one. Yet before Yorkshire folk do too much finger-pointing, they should remember the circumstances in which they signed Rhodes. It's said that he was chosen ahead of another spinner, Albert Cordingly, on the toss of a coin.

Rhodes was a shoe-in for the England Test side – for whom, incidentally, he batted in all 11 positions (a feat shared by Vinoo Mankad for India). In the county game, he became such a fixture for Yorkshire that other slow bowlers on their books couldn't get a look-in.

In the 1920s, another young prospect headed south for Warwickshire and, once again, was given a trial. The coaches looked him over in the nets, ummed and aahed and sent him home. Surely they'd learnt their lesson this time? Er, no, actually. This time the reject was Hedley Verity, another of the true pre-war English greats. A slow-medium left-armer, Verity soon became a worthy successor to Rhodes at Yorkshire and in ten seasons took 1,956 first-class wickets at an average of 14.87. In his 40 Tests, he took a total of 144 wickets at an average of 24.37, and he remains the only player to have taken 14 Test wickets in a single day. He remains the most economic English Test bowler ever (see page 127) and in 1934 at Lords claimed 15 for 104, so sharing with Rhodes the record at that time for the most wickets in an Ashes Test.

Comparisons between cricketers tend to be meaningless but in assessing Verity's talent you have only to read the words of Sir Don Bradman, whose average in 46 innings against England was 91.42. When asked about the relative merits of Verity and Australia's masterful spinner Clarrie Grimmett, Bradman was typically frank. 'I think I know all about Clarrie,' he said, 'but with Hedley I am never sure. You see, there's no breaking point with him.'

Obtaining the services of Rhodes and Verity on the rebound gave Yorkshire bragging rights for many a year. All was well until 1946, when a Bradford-born off-spinner who'd played for the county's colts realised that, despite high praise from the likes of South African skipper Dudley Nourse, he wasn't going to break through. The lad then signed for Surrey – but only after officials at The Oval had checked with Yorkshire to make sure they were happy. 'Nah, go ahead,' said Headingley. 'We don't want Jim Laker.'

Ten years later, playing against the Australians at Old Trafford, Laker took 9 for 37 in the first innings and 10 for 53 in the second. No other bowler in history has ever taken more than 17 wickets in a first-class match, never mind a Test. Laker finished his first-class career with 1,944 scalps, at an average of 18.41.

— LACKING TECHNIQUE —

Of course, you say, the inability to spot cricketing talent couldn't happen today. There are more coaches than ever, better qualified than ever, and all clubs have structures in place to identify and nurture potential stars. Take the case of West Lothian Cricket Club, who in 1988 wanted an up-and-coming young West Indian player to help coach their colts and give their league side a boost.

On the advice of a Caribbean scout, they appointed a slow bowler named Jerry Angus (who went on to take 21 wickets for Guyana). The scout had also checked out a 19-year-old batsman but reported that he lacked the technique and stamina necessary for a big innings. Neither did he show enough natural ability for those damp, treacherous Scottish wickets.

The batsman's name? Brian Lara, the man who holds the world-record test score of 400 (against England in Antigua, 2004). The man who became the first player in Test match history to hold the record for the highest individual innings twice. The man who is only the second player in history (behind the legendary Sir Don) to score two triple Test 100s in his career, and who stands joint-second with Wally Hammond as scorer of most Test double centuries. If only he'd worked harder on his stamina and technique.

'I suppose it was an error of judgement of some magnitude and makes me look a bit silly,' said West Lothian selection committee member Gordon Hollins in one interview. 'Jerry Angus stayed with us for two seasons and was very good. However, Lara really is something else, a phenomenal batsman, almost freakish in the range of boundary shots he can play. The better he gets, the more he will haunt me. I can't remember the name of the scout in Trinidad now, but I know we gave him the sack.'

— WALLY'S JOLLY —

There have been plenty of one-sided Ashes matches in recent years – usually in Australia's favour – so it's refreshing to turn the clock back to 1938 and the biggest 'no contest' of the lot. By the fifth and final Test at The Oval that year, Australia were 1–0 up and had already retained the Ashes. Even so, the rubber was at stake, and when Wally Hammond won the toss, he and his team were determined not to let the Aussies leave the field as overall victors.

Hammond decided to bat…and bat…and then bat a bit more. In fact, the tourists bowled 335.2 overs by the time he declared on a trifling 903 for 7, an innings that saw Len Hutton contribute a ruthless 364. Understandably, the Australians were in no mood for a scrap – especially since their prolific run-makers Jack Fingleton (pulled muscle) and Don Bradman (broken ankle) were confined to barracks. They stuttered to 201 in their first innings and raised the white flag with just 123 in their second. England won by an innings and 579 runs – still the greatest margin in the history of Test cricket. The Aussies gratefully sailed home. Those were the days.

— MEAN MACHINES —

The following table lists bowlers with the best Test-career economy rates (ie runs conceded per over). It's interesting to note that the last player to enter the top ten was Ray Illingworth, over 30 years ago. This isn't to say that today's bowlers are less skilled; rather, that runs per over have increased with more aggressive batting. Few punters now would bet on Trevor Goddard losing top spot!

Economy	Bowler and Era	Team	Tests	Overs	Runs Conceded	Wickets	Average
1.64	Trevor Goddard, 1955–70	SA	41	1,956	3,226	123	26.22

ECONOMY	BOWLER AND ERA	TEAM	TESTS	OVERS	RUNS CONCEDED	WICKETS	AVERAGE
1.67	Bapu Nadkarni, 1955–68	Ind	41	1,527	2,559	88	29.07
1.78	Ken Mackay, 1956–63	Aus	37	965	1,721	50	34.42
1.82	Gerry Gomez, 1939–54	WI	29	872	1,590	58	27.41
1.88	Hedley Verity, 1931–9	Eng	40	1,862	3,510	144	24.37
1.89	Johnny Wardle, 1947–57	Eng	28	1,099	2,080	102	20.39
1.90	Denis Atkinson, 1948–58	WI	22	866	1,647	47	35.04
1.91	Ray Illingworth, 1958–73	Eng	61	1,989	3,807	122	31.20
1.93	Charlie Turner, 1886–95	Aus	17	863	1,670	101	16.53
1.94	Maurice Tate, 1924–35	Eng	39	2,087	4,055	155	26.16

— CHEAP HAULS —

Career averages may be the definitive assessment of a bowler's ability but nothing warms the spectator's heart quite like a glorious one-off performance. Here are the best (ie cheapest) Test hauls, from nine-fors to five-fors. George Lohmann must have enjoyed his trip to South Africa!

NAME	TEAM	WICKETS	RUNS CONCEDED	OPPONENT	VENUE AND SERIES
G Lohmann	England	9	28	South Africa	Johannesburg, 1895/6
G Lohmann	England	8	7	S Africa	Port Elizabeth 1895/6
S Harmison	England	7	12	West Indies	Kingston 2004
J Lawson	West Indies	6	3	Bangaldsh	Chittagong 2002/3
E Toshack	Australia	5	2	India	Brisbane 1947/48

— LEADING WICKET-TAKERS *—

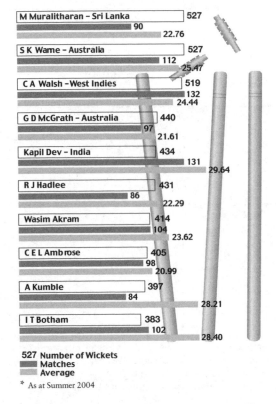

	Number of Wickets	Matches	Average
M Muralitharan – Sri Lanka	527	90	22.76
S K Warne – Australia	527	112	25.47
C A Walsh – West Indies	519	132	24.44
G D McGrath – Australia	440	97	21.61
Kapil Dev – India	434	131	29.64
R J Hadlee	431	86	22.29
Wasim Akram	414	104	23.62
C E L Ambrose	405	98	20.99
A Kumble	397	84	28.21
I T Botham	383	102	28.40

527 Number of Wickets
Matches
Average

* As at Summer 2004

— CRICKET, TRIVIA AND TRUE HEROES —

It could be argued that professional cricket is a trivial pursuit played by people who can't get proper jobs, and yet the qualities that produce outstanding players – determination, doggedness and a desire to win – also mould great national heroes. Many cricketers served their country bravely during two world wars, but two names particularly come to mind: Hedley Verity, he of the unspotted genius (see page 124), and Geoff Edrich, of a remarkable Norfolk cricketing dynasty. Edrich's father, Bill, was a Norfolk Club player; his Aunt

Alice captained the Norfolk Ladies team; two of his brothers won county caps – Eric (Lancashire) and Brian (Kent) – and the third, WJ Edrich ('Bill Jnr'), played for both Middlesex and England (39 times). Their younger cousin, John, later became one of the few truly outstanding English batsmen of the 1960s and 1970s.

Geoff Edrich was about to be signed by Hampshire when World War II broke out. He fought as a sergeant in the Far East, and in 1942 he was taken prisoner by the Japanese at the fall of Singapore. Despite suffering horrendous conditions in his Changi PoW camp, he helped to boost the morale of British and Australian prisoners by organising a 'Test' series on the rest days, which came around every three weeks. 'Australia' was captained by the real Australian Test wicket-keeper Ben Barnett, but England took the three-match series thanks to three consecutive centuries from Geoff.

Edrich was later forced to work on the notorious 'Railroad of Death' in Thailand, an ordeal which only six members of his platoon survived, and weighed barely six stone when he was liberated. Yet by 1946 he had recovered sufficiently to win his county cap for Lancashire, the start of a first-class career in which he amassed 15,600 runs, averaged 34.82 and took 333 catches.

Hedley Verity's cricket career was outlined earlier, but the manner of his death says far more about the man. In 1943 he was a captain in the Green Howards as the Eighth Army launched the first of its attacks on German-held positions at Catania, Sicily. Verity led his company for 1,000 yards through blazing cornfields as tracer fire, mortars and firebombs rained down.

He identified a farmhouse as the enemy stronghold and was in the process of attacking it when he was struck and mortally wounded in the chest. 'Keep going,' he told his men, 'and get them out of that house.' The assault failed. Captain Verity's troops last saw him dying in front of the smouldering corn, his head cradled by his batman. Rather puts cricket in perspective, doesn't it?

— OUT, MANKADED —

Few players achieve such fame, or notoriety, that their name becomes a cricketing verb. One exception is the fiercely competitive Indian all-rounder Vinoo Mankad, who in the 1947 second Test at Sydney famously ran out Australia's Bill Brown for backing up (ie creeping down the pitch to steal a run) at the non-striker's end. Whenever this has happened since, Australians know it as the act of being 'Mankaded'.

Etiquette of course dictates that a bowler should always warn a transgressing batsman once before whipping off the bails. As far as Vinoo was concerned, though, Brown *had* been warned; he'd just forgotten about it. Hardly surprising, really; that warning was given during a game the previous month.

— SWING KING —

In the early 1990s, cricket supporters were hit by a baffling new phrase in the lexicon of media pundits. 'Reverse swing' was quite the thing and although few ordinary mortals had a clue what it was, everyone knew who'd perfected it. His name was Waqar Younis, otherwise known as the Burewala Express, and with his partner, Wasim Akram, he would give Pakistan the most feared strike-bowling partnership in world cricket.

As we know, the ability to make a cricket ball swing depends on several factors, most importantly the variation of air movement across the rough and shiny sides of the ball. It usually works best when the cherry is new, but it can also appear when an old ball is rough on both sides. In this event, the bowler's grip and action remains the same but the ball starts to swing the opposite way – ie in 'reverse'. Waqar discovered he had a knack for this delivery, serving up in-swingers designed to hit batsmen's toes or leg stump – whichever came first – at 90mph. It will surprise none of his victims that more than 29 per cent of his wickets were lbws, while 27 per cent were bowled.

When Waqar got everything right, he was unplayable, and 1992 holds some particularly miserable memories for England. Waqar and Wasim had them at 4 for 1 in the Lord's Test, 8 for 28 at Headingley and 7 for 25 at The Oval, débâcles that occurred during a three-year spell in which Waqar was unquestionably the bowler batsmen least liked to face. In that time he took 109 wickets at 18.07, with an amazing strike rate of 33.55.

After becoming Pakistan's captain, Waqar came back for another go at humiliating England, taking 7 for 36 in an ODI at Headingley in 2001. Sadly he stayed in the top flight a little too long, and when Australia humbled Pakistan at Sharjah in October 2002 – reducing them to 59 and 53 all out – it was on his watch. An horrendous World Cup followed, in which Pakistan managed to beat only Holland and Namibia, and Waqar announced his retirement in April 2004.

Wasim and Waqar pass into cricket history as one of the truly great fast-bowling partnerships, yet in their 14 years together they became like a crotchety old married couple with some all-too-public spats. In 1993 Wasim claimed that his first captaincy was sabotaged by Waqar's dressing-room politicking, and by that 2001 tour things had got so bad that Wasim needed the casting vote of the Pakistan Board chairman to get on the plane.

— WASIM'S WEAKNESS —

It wasn't just opposing batsmen who shuddered at the sight of Wasim Akram taking the field. Team-mates were none too keen on batting with him on account of his erratic – no, let's be honest, appalling – running between the wickets. No other international cricketer has been run out more often – seven times in Test matches and 38 times in ODIs. It was rumoured that batsmen at the non-striker's end would sometimes scream, 'No!' at Wasim before the ball had even pitched. He didn't care. No other player has ever matched his record of 300 wickets and 3,000 runs in ODIs

— MARK, IT'S PETER —

Just occasionally, the pomposity of professional sport is punctured by a good old-fashioned, grade-one cock-up. Who can forget that bizarre moment in 1984 when, on the fourth evening of the second Test between England and the West Indies, England's Allan Lamb and Paul Downton were offered the light and purposefully strolled off.

It was a puzzling decision because England had fought themselves into a winning position with a 300-plus lead. They desperately needed quick runs to stand a chance of bowling the tourists out and levelling the five-match series at 1–1. Still more puzzling was that England's captain, David Gower, appeared to have gone AWOL. Why wasn't he on the balcony, watching, assessing and gesturing for his troops to jolly well battle on through the gloom? Answer: He was watching Wimbledon on the dressing-room TV. The West Indies reached England's target of 342 the following day and won the series 5–0.

Three years later, it was Gower's successor, Mike Gatting, who blushed hard when he missed the umpires' call to lead his team onto the field for an afternoon session against Pakistan. Fair enough, really; the England lads are surely entitled to watch the 4:30 at Ascot.

Sometimes a cock-up can re-invent itself as a triumph. Before the final Test of the 1986/7 Ashes series, cricket hacks got onto a leak from the Australian selectors that Mark Taylor had been called up. As the vacancy was for an opener, and future Aussie captain Taylor had been extensively tipped as a possible Test opener, the press pack not unreasonably descended on him for a reaction. However, when the formal announcement was made, the Taylor on the team sheet carried the initial P, not M. Shurely shome mishtake? The only P Taylor anyone could think of was Peter Taylor, but he was an off-spinner, not an opening bat. Besides, he'd turned out only once for his state side, New South Wales, that season.

The Australian selectors insisted there had been no mix-up. England had already won the rubber, so it could be argued that this was the time for experimentation. Even so, replacing an opener with an inexperienced, under-played off-spinner was distinctly odd, given that the Australians take no Test match lightly. Especially against the old enemy.

As it turned out, Peter Taylor answered the critics, bowling superbly to post figures of 6–78 and helping the Aussies to record their only Test win of the series.

— UMPIRE SIGNALS —

Four runs

Six runs

Wide

Bye

Leg bye

No ball

Out

Short run

Dead ball

— A CENTURY OF CAPTAINCY BLUNDERS —

1900   SAMMY WOODS – Woods's Gentlemen had amassed such a bumper score that he loftily ordered his batsmen to get themselves out so that he could have a bowl at the Players. The Players reached their target of 501 the following day with two wickets to spare.

1911   JOHNNY DOUGLAS – Douglas was a dangerous opening bowler on his day, but he suffered from the classic weakness of captains who bowl – namely, a failure to recognise his bad days. The first Ashes Test in Sydney was a case in point. Douglas, standing in for a sick Plum Warner, opened with himself and Frank Foster, even though the great Sydney Barnes was available. Douglas took a miserable 1–62, and when he finally chucked the cherry to Barnes it was returned with the immortal words, 'You've bowled 'em in, now you bowl 'em out.' Douglas made matters worse by failing to open his batting with Jack Hobbs and Wilfred Rhodes. England lost the match but went on to win the series decisively, with Foster and Barnes sharing 55 wickets between them.

1930   THE HON FREDERICK SOMERSET GOUGH CALTHORPE – The Hon Frederick's side scored a ludicrous 849 in the first innings of a timeless test against the West Indies at Sabina Park, thanks largely to the first triple century in Test cricket from Andy Sandham. Having bowled the home side out for just 286, the Hon Fred then even more ludicrously failed to enforce the follow-on. He eventually ran out of time because he had to catch the boat home, proving that, as well as being a hopeless Test player (average 18.42 with the bat, 91 with the ball), he was also a spectacularly useless captain. His background failed to save him and he never played for England again.

1930   PERCY CHAPMAN – Things didn't quite go according to plan for Calthorpe's successor when he took the helm for a home Ashes series. In the third Test at Headingley, Chapman's strategy for dealing with Don Bradman was to set attacking fields, bowl 22 overs per hour and get the little wizard out, rather than attempt to contain him. At the end of day one, it was time for plan B. Bradman walked off undefeated on 309 and went on to score a then world-record 334.

1946   WALLY HAMMOND – Batting genius he may have been, but Hammond was neither a tactician nor a leader. He was horribly exposed after winning the toss in the second Ashes Test at Sydney, instructing his batsmen to remain in the crease against Australia's spinners. Ian Johnson and the wonderfully named Colin McCool then gleefully set about England's batsmen, tossing the ball ever higher to lure them forward. Johnson finished with 8–134 in the match off 59 overs, including an 11-over spell in which just three singles were scored. McCool registered 8–182 off 55. England lost the game and the series.

1954   LEN HUTTON – After winning the toss for the first Test at Brisbane, Hutton became the first English captain since Johnny Douglas in 1912 to put Australia in to bat. Bad idea. Bedser, Statham, Tyson and Bailey each conceded well over 100 runs apiece, and by the end of day three England's response to their hosts' 601–8, declared, was 107–5. Australia won by an innings and 154 runs.

1963   TED DEXTER – With England defending a modest first-innings score of 279 in the third Test at Sydney, Dexter unaccountably decided to attack debutant batsman Barry Shepherd with the (very) gentle leg breaks of (very) occasional bowler Ken Barrington. Barrington conceded 43 runs off 8 overs, Shepherd finished 71 not out, and Australia posted a 40-run first-innings lead to speed them to victory and, as it turned out, retention of the Ashes. Opposition batsman Norm O'Neill referred to Barrington's spell as 'one of Dexter's biggest tactical blunders of the series'. Just how many others did Norm count?

1985   KAPIL DEV – Given the talent at his disposal, Dev looked certain to guide India to their first series win in Australia, especially since the hosts had just lost a series to New Zealand for the first time. The bubbly was on ice by the final day of the second Test, with the Aussies just 45 runs ahead and two wickets left. Unfortunately, one of them was skipper and chief party-spoiler Alan Border. Dev made the classic mistake of letting Border take singles to expose the tail-enders, and although he got Bruce Reid for 13, last man Dave Gilbert had forgotten to read the script. Gilbert and Border put on 77, used up two precious hours in the process and ensured that India were left stranded on 59–2, just 67 short of victory, when rain intervened. The three-Test series finished 0–0.

1994   MICHAEL ATHERTON – Athers won the toss for the third ODI against West Indies at Kingstown, St Vincent, and was pondering his decision

— A CENTURY OF CAPTAINCY (CONT'D) —

when 'a local Rastafarian with a huge spliff' urged him to bat while the tide was out. Atherton rejected this counsel, put West Indies in and watched Haynes, Simmons, Lara and Co. post a massive 313. That secured a 165-run win, which at the time was the heaviest defeat ever suffered by England in 222 ODIs.

2002   NASSER HUSSAIN – Hussain started his doomed Ashes campaign in Brisbane with the worst possible decision: putting Australia in to bat. By the end of the first day, the score was 364–2, with Matthew Hayden undefeated on 186. England did manage some kind of fightback in their first innings, but it was all too late. 'To me, Hussain's choice meant England didn't want to expose their batting and thought bowling was the safe option,' said Australian skipper Steve Waugh afterwards. Too right; in their second innings, Nasser's boys were blown away for 79.

— CAP THAT —

Herbert Sutcliffe didn't win his England cap until he was 29 and then highlighted the selectors' shame by belting 4,555 runs over 54 Tests. No other England batsman with a minimum of 500 runs has ever topped his 60.73 batting average. Sutcliffe was also the first person to hit four 100s in a Test series (against Australia) and was one half of England's greatest opening partnership. The other half is featured below.

— THE MASTER —

Not for nothing was Jack Hobbs known as 'the Master'. He was, is and always will be cricket's most prolific batsman, with 61,237 first-class runs and 197 centuries to his name. God alone knows how many more he would have struck but for the Great War and his habit of getting himself out after posting a century to let someone else have a go. More than half his 100s came when he'd passed the age of 40, and at 50 he became the oldest man to score a Test century – another record that will never be broken.

He was also the first professional cricketer to receive a knighthood.

There are many stories about his charm, comradeship and loyalty, but Hobbs was also one of the kindest men in the game, who remembered how it felt to be a young player starting out. A typical story concerns his intervention to end the embarrassment of his Surrey team-mate Alf Gover, who in 1928 was emerging as a fiery quick bowler. In the dressing room, Gover was approached by the irrepressible practical joker Patsy Hendren, batting for local rivals Middlesex. 'Go easy with the short stuff,' Hendren pleaded, 'I'm not as young as I was.'

No county fast bowler – let alone Gover – was going to be told how to bowl, and his first three deliveries were all bouncers. The 'doddering' Hendren ate them for breakfast, hooking the first two for four and the third for a six. As Gover trudged disconsolately back to his mark, the Master jogged alongside. 'He may be old,' said Hobbs, 'but he's the best player of fast bowling in England.' Gover switched to line and length.

— PATSY'S PRANK —

Patsy Hendren's sense of fun was often wicked but invariably funny. One morning, after a long night in the bar, he and his fellow not-out batsman Jack Hearne were due to resume play when Hearne confessed that he still felt a bit woozy. Would Patsy possibly mind helping him out to the middle? 'Delighted,' said Patsy, and off they strolled.

When they reached their destination, Hearne couldn't see anyone around. 'Any chance of a sit-down, Patsy?' he pleaded. 'Oh, why not?' said Hendren casually. 'We're the only ones here so far.' He was right as well; while Hearne lay back gratefully on the grass Hendren, quietly slipped away to join the umpires and fielders, standing stony-faced 50 yards away beside the wicket.

— TOSS LORE —

Earlier the science of coin-tossing was investigated, but this simple act is also steeped in cricketing folklore. Dr WG Grace once urged all captains, 'Take what the gods have offered. When you win the toss, always bat. If the conditions suit bowling, think about it. Then always bat.' Richie Benaud's edict is tougher to follow: 'The mark of a great captain is the ability to win the toss at the right time.'

It's a strange thing, but neither of them is quite right – at least, not according to an exhaustive analysis by the Aussie-based website Howstat.com. Howstat looked at all 998 Test matches up to the end of 2001 and weeded out any that didn't end in a result (ie those drawn or tied). They established how often a toss-winning side went on to win a match, the relative successes of home and touring toss winners, and the statistical advantages of electing to bat or field. (Frightening, isn't it?) Their conclusions are as follows. Bear in mind that home sides win Tests 59.62 per cent of the time, regardless, so any toss advantage has to be set against that yardstick.

	WON MATCHES	LOST MATCHES
SIDE WINNING TOSS (OVERALL)	53.14% (525)	46.86% (463)
HOME SIDE WINNING TOSS	61.89% (328)	38.11% (202)
TOURISTS WINNING TOSS	43.01% (197)	56.99% (261)

There were 740 occasions on which a toss-winning captain elected to bat and the match ended in a result:

	WON MATCHES	LOST MATCHES
ELECTING TO BAT (OVERALL)	52.97% (392)	47.03% (348)
ELECTING TO BAT (HOME SIDE)	60.31% (237)	36.69% (156)
ELECTING TO BAT (TOURISTS)	44.67% (155)	55.33% (192)

There were 248 occasions on which a toss-winning captain put the opposition in and the match ended in a result:

	WON MATCHES	LOST MATCHES
PUTTING OPPONENTS IN (OVERALL)	53.63% (133)	46.37% (115)
PUTTING OPPONENTS IN (HOME CAPTAIN'S DECISION)	66.42% (91)	33.58% (46)
PUTTING OPPONENT'S IN (AWAY CAPTAIN'S DECISION)	37.84% (42)	63.16% (69)

The sad truth for Mssrs Benaud, Grace and a good few other sages is that, apart from the rare times a wicket has been under-prepared (deliberately or otherwise), winning the toss offers only a marginal advantage. For the home side, it works best when they send the opposition in (a 6.8 per cent improvement on overall odds), and for tourists it helps to bat first (a 4.29 per cent improvement). Touring skippers should not, statistically speaking, ever win the toss and insert their hosts; when they do, their chance of a win dips to 37.84 per cent. But we knew that anyway. Didn't we, Nasser?

— BACK TO BACK —

Only two cricketers have ever managed to score centuries in both innings of their debut Test match. Step forward Lawrence Rowe, of the West Indies, who got 214 and 100 not out against New Zealand at Kingstown in February 1972, and Pakistan's Yasir Hameed, who hit 170 and 105 off Bangladesh at Karachi in August 2003.

Six batsman have managed to score centuries on both their home and tour debuts, most recently England's Andrew Strauss, who got 112 at Lord's and 126 at Port Elizabeth in 2004. Michael Clarke of Australia managed the same feat that year, with 151 at Bangalore and 141 in Brisbane. For the record, the others are Pakistan's Azhar Mahmood (128 and 136, both against South Africa); Kepler Wessels for his adopted Australia (162 vs England and 141 vs Sri Lanka); Lawrence Rowe (who matched his 214 with a 107 in Australia); KS Ranjitsinhji, the Indian prince who played for England at the end of the 19th century (154 and 175, both against Australia); and, first of the bunch, Harry 'Little Dasher' Graham, of Australia (107 and 105, both against England).

— ALL DOWNHILL —

Sports people never seem to learn the lesson about quitting at the top before age, or fate, brings them down. Indian spinner Nilesh Kulkarni is a case in point. After taking Atapattu's wicket with his first ball in Test cricket at Colombo in 1997 (the 12th time a debutant has managed it, by the way), he should have felt a twinge in the hamstring, asked to be taken off and somehow made himself unavailable for selection thereafter. That way he could have stayed in the record book with a Test wicket every ball. Alas, Nilesh carried on, finished with 1–195 in the match, got 0–67 in his next Test and 1–70 in his third and last. As of 2001, his bowling average stood at 166.

— BOTH RECORDS —

Two cricketing feats – the most times anyone has scored 100 runs and taken five wickets in a Test, and the shortest number of Tests to score 1,000 runs and take 100 wickets – were achieved by the same man. It's not hard to guess who. England's greatest all-rounder and most famous living cricketer, Ian Terence Botham, did this kind of stuff in between eating three Shredded Wheats for breakfast.

Just for the record, Botham managed five-plus-a-century on six occasions, two of which came in the same match against India in 1980. Amazingly, he took just 21 Tests to bag 100 wickets and 1,000 runs, producing averages of 4.76 and 47.6 respectively.

— CLASS OF '81 —

Whatever all-rounder Andrew Flintoff achieves in his career, he will always be compared to Beefy. This is dreadfully unfair, since the odds against *anyone* ever emulating Botham's role in the 1981 Ashes series are so long as to be incalculable.

If you recall, Beefy had just quit the captaincy and was looking to take it out on someone. He first brutalised the tourists at Headingley with 149, setting up Bob Willis for a devastating match-winning spell of 8–43 to bring the series level at 1–1. Willis was then England's fastest post-war bowler since Frank Tyson, and with his mad axeman's stare, wild hair and maniacal arm-pumping, he was also more scary.

In the next Test, England were about to lose when Botham stepped up to produce figures of 5–1 and secure the win. By the time the show got to Old Trafford, the Australians had a plan to keep him quiet, which proved to be not terribly good when a feisty Botham hit a technically perfect 118. In fact, it wasn't quite technically perfect, since at times he appeared to be using a sixth sense; twice during that century he disdainfully swatted Dennis Lillee for six over fine leg. Replays show he wasn't even watching the ball.

Approaching his 50th year (2005), Botham – now a Sky TV commentator – may have lost his awesome natural ability, but feisty? He still does feisty. The ICC's insistence on England's tour to Zimbabwe, combined with its bent-arm bowling changes, drew the following observation: 'Once again, the ICC have shown themselves to be weak, pathetic and useless. They have been tinkering with laws of the game which have served cricket well for more than 100 years while turning a blind eye to atrocities in one of their own member countries.' If you see him at the bar, don't start him up.

— WELL ROUNDED —

Cricket trivia worshippers, or 'sweaters' (anoraks really belong in soccer), will forever debate the relative merits of all-rounders. Looking strictly at the stats however, the only real argument is between the great Sir Garry Sobers and Jacques Kallis. To settle this, one possible formula is to subtract a player's bowling average (ie the number of wickets per runs conceded) from his batting average (the number of runs, divided by the number of dismissals) to calculate a 'super average'.

The league table below lists the top eight all-rounders, as at November 2004. Of the current crop, Jacques Kallis is there of right, but Shaun Pollock and Sanath Jayasuriya are included because they clearly have opportunities for advancement. Bad news for Botham and Flintoff fans, though: Botham's super average is 5.14 (33.54 minus 28.40), while ahead of England's 2004/5 South African tour Flintoff's stood at minus 4.42 (32.98 minus 37.40).

The 'worst' all-rounders using this calculation are New Zealand's Dipak Patel, on minus 21.36 (20.69 minus 42.05), and India's Madan Lal, on minus 17.43 (22.65 minus 40.08).

NAME	BATTING AVERAGE	BOWLING AVERAGE	SUPER AVERAGE
Garry Sobers	57.78	34.04	23.75
Jacques Kallis	53.85	30.68	23.17
Wally Hammond	58.45	37.80	20.65
Imran Khan	37.69	22.81	14.88
Aubrey Faulkner	40.79	26.58	14.21
Keith Miller	36.97	22.97	14.00
Shaun Pollock	33.06	21.56	11.50
Sanath Jayasuriya	43.45	32.26	11.19

— MAKES YOU WEEP —

What have former Australian captain Kim Hughes and retired England skipper Nasser Hussain got in common? They both tend to get tearful. In 1984, Hughes broke down at a press conference after resigning (the West Indies had just blown his side away in the second Test at Brisbane) and never recovered his golden-boy status. He scored two runs in his next four innings and then abandoned ship completely by leading a rebel side to South Africa.

Nasser quit in an altogether more satisfying manner – his undefeated century to beat New Zealand at Lord's in 2004 – but still got caught up in the emotion of the moment. 'I was willing to fight against [my age] and opposition and the people who were writing me off,' he said, 'but not against youth.' That's when he started blubbing, just like Hughes.

— FIELDING POSITIONS —

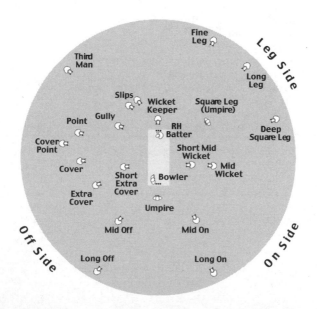

— COACHING THE CHUCK —

The international row over chucking has had a big impact at youth and club level, nowhere more so than in Devon, where distinguished county youth coach Roger Mann has campaigned for years for the right to teach a bent-arm bowling action he calls 'elbow spin'.

However, when in early 2004 Mr Mann announced plans to begin coaching the technique at schoolboy level, there was uproar among traditionalists. The Devon Cricket Umpires' and Scorers' Association published a thinly veiled accusation that young players would be schooled in the art of cheating. The issue was particularly sensitive given the dark mutterings surrounding the Devon Premier League's leading wicket-taker for the previous three seasons: Aqeel Ahmed of Barton Cricket Club. Opposing batsmen convinced themselves that he was 'doing a Murali'.

Mr Mann, vice-chair of the Devon Schools' Cricket Association and an ECB Level II coach, told journalists that he'd completed an experimental course for older players 'in an effort to persuade our local umpires to be decisive.' A coaching programme for children, he said, would follow. 'Boys see Muralitharan taking 500 wickets and ask, "Why can't I bowl like him? Why do I have to bowl like [England spinner] Gareth Batty?"' said Mr Mann. 'One umpire has told me it would be a brave man to "call" a bowler during a local league match. That's terribly frustrating for me as a coach. If this action is illegal under the laws, they should stop it. If it's not, I want to coach it. I don't mind either way, but the situation at the moment is fudge and nonsense.'

In a letter to the ECB's performance director at Lord's, Hugh Morris, Mr Mann claimed that the Devon CUSA 'has an understanding between its members to overlook the legality of the action at this level, preferring to leave the decision to others'.

However, Devon umpires hit back in their newsletter *Scoring*, in which an editorial pointed out that, 'If the first-class game and ICC cannot agree on some of their players, what chance do we amateurs stand? …Are we being told that this coach is deliberately encouraging and teaching players to cheat? What about the Spirit of Cricket?'

Hopefully, the new interpretation of Law 24 (see page 146–7) will smooth things over. Time to buy a protractor.

— THAT'S PANTS —

The cricketing world and his dog celebrated when Brian Lara posted his world-record score against Durham in 1994, although the smiles looked a little fixed on the faces of marketing wallahs from his sponsor, Joe Bloggs Jeans. Why? Because Lara's 501 perfectly matched the brand of their deadly rivals, Levi's 501. As one agonised Bloggs executive later conceded, 'It would have been better if he'd scored one more.'

— BAILS TO THAT! —

A little something from the betcha-can't-do-that-again archives. In a 1975 county match, Leicestershire captain Ray Illingworth saw his wicket-keeper, Barry Dudleston, miss a straightforward stumping chance to dismiss the dangerous Lancashire batsman and future England coach David Lloyd. A few overs later, a grumpy – and incredulous – Illingworth saw Dudleston attempt another stumping. This time the bails *did* fly off…only to land safely back on the stump sockets. That's a great big not out! Lloyd went on to make an unbeaten century and secure the draw.

— UNSAFE KEEPING —

They say you have to be mad to be a goalkeeper, and the same is true for wicket-keepers. Aside from one or two brilliant catches in a career, nobody ever remembers the diving stops down leg side or the tricky 90mph take an inch off the ground in the final over of a sweltering session. Drop a couple of sitters or do a Dudleston, though, and you're history.

Just ask poor Parthiv Patel. As he and his side drove into Bombay for the final Test of the already-dead 2004 series between India and Australia, he was greeted by a 40-foot-high advertising hoarding cruelly depicting him as a hapless cartoon character. The caption read, 'Parthetic'.

Patel had certainly been trying out ball-repellent gloves for a few Tests, and his failure to swallow a chance given by Matthew Hayden – then on nought – in the Madras Test was the kind of blunder that drags a whole team down. Even so, cricket is a team game. India supporters may have been furious at losing their first home rubber against the Aussies since 1969, but one Patel doesn't lose a series.

— SANDWICH BAN —

South Africa spent much of 2003 and 2004 in turmoil, subsiding from second to sixth in the Test rankings, and from second to eighth in the ODI table. It was hard enough being ejected from their own World Cup at the pool stage, but a losing streak that included ten ODIs in 2004 forced the United Cricket Board's hand. The calm and reserved coach Eric Simons was replaced by the loud and abrasive Ray Jennings. Actually, Jennings was second choice; they couldn't get Homer Simpson.

Jennings, who played 159 first-class matches in the 1970s and 1980s as a wicket-keeper bat, has the most unorthodox coaching approach in world cricket. At home he cut his teeth on the unfashionable Easterns side, bolstering promising youngsters with top pros like Daryll Cullinan and Andrew Hall. The formula worked, and in 2002 Easterns beat a Western Province team oozing international class in the SuperSport series final.

There's nothing unorthodox about mixing young and old blood, but the Jennings manual on incentive and discipline is rather more radical. He once threw the Easterns players' sandwiches out of their dressing room and, on another occasion, offered his fast bowlers 1,000 rand (around £80) for every opponent they could fell with a bouncer. That only came to light when young André Nel hit Allan Donald on the head and immediately burst into tears. Donald was his boyhood hero. Jennings ordered Nel not to apologise.

After taking the helm of South Africa's A side, Jennings made clear that anyone bowling no-balls or wides would do laps of the pitch. On tour in Zimbabwe, he punished players by clearing the team fridge – complete with energy drinks – out of the dressing room and making everyone drink warm water. Yet his other mantra suggests that failing is fine. 'I don't want the guys to be scared of failing,' he said on accepting his new job. 'I want them to fail. Life is about failing. It's the way you learn.' It could have been Homer talking.

— GIVING GLEN THE BIRD —

Teasing Glenn McGrath is not necessarily the brightest thing for a cricketer to do, so you have to hand it to McGrath's New South Wales colleague Brad McNamara for christening him 'Pidge'. Apparently, on their first day's training together, McNamara took one look at his new team-mate's long, thin, white legs encased in shorts and spluttered, 'You've stolen those from a pigeon!' The nickname stuck…but not everyone uses it.

— CHUCKED A LIFELINE —

Bad news for sledgers. Everyone knows there are few jibes that wind up a bowler more than the scathing 'You're a chucker.' Occasionally, other words are inserted between 'a' and 'chucker', but the sentiment is the same.

Now the ICC has put the mockers on this gratifying insult by officially ruling that *everyone's* a chucker, except the West Indies' Ramnaresh Sarwan. And not just current players, either; in addition to the known dodgy actions of 1960s quicks such as Charlie Griffith (called 11 times while bowling for the Windies in the 1960 Lord's Test), South Africa's Geoff Griffin, New Zealand's Gary Bartlett and Australia's Ian Meckiff and Gordon Rorke, you can also add 'gold standard' actions like – gulp – Fred Trueman's.

So what's going on? Law 24, Section 2, of the ICC rule book insists that 'A ball is fairly delivered in respect to the arm if, once the bowler's arm has reached the level of the shoulder in the delivery swing, the elbow joint is not straightened partially or completely from that point until the ball has left the hand.' That's fairly clear – once you've re-read it a few times – but in recent years it has become unenforceable. The International Cricket Council eventually decided there would be a 'tolerance' for arm-straightening of five degrees for spinners, seven and a half for medium pacers and ten for fast bowlers.

By 2000, it was obvious that this had solved nothing. The row focused (unfairly) on Muttiah Muralitharan, whose 'doosra' ball (an off spinner delivered like a wristy leg-break) was seen as potentially illegal. The ICC asked him not to use it until biotechnicians had analysed other bowlers' actions. Few could forget how, at the MCG on Boxing Day 1995, Australian umpire Darrell Hair cancelled Christmas goodwill and called Murali seven times in three overs.

Muralitharan has always insisted that a deformed elbow prevents him from doing things differently. In fact, deformed or not, he appears to be in good company. The secret 18-month biotech investigation analysed 34 deliveries from 21 bowlers during first-class matches in Australia and the ICC Champions' Trophy. High-speed cameras with zoom lenses proved that *every single* ball was chucked under the strict interpretation of Law 23. Fourteen of them involved arm-straightening of more than 10 per cent and five of more than 15 per cent. One chap managed 22 per cent. Only Jan Zelezny* throws better.

Further analysis showed that some bowlers complicated the issue by hyperextending their elbow backwards – effectively bending it the wrong way during delivery. The only answer to that, said the analysts, was surgery. However, they also proved that arms must bend *more* than 15 degrees to achieve a meaningful advantage. At that point, average delivery speeds climb above 140kmh (87mph), the level at which even top-class batsman have problems.

The scientists showed that Muralitharan's arm was significantly straighter than several other big-name bowlers tested. His standard off-break has a mere five-degree bend, while even his doosra is down to 10.2 degrees, thanks to a modified, straighter run-up. At the time of writing, the ICC is expected to rubber-stamp a new interpretation of Law 24 allowing a 'flat-rate' 15-degree flex for all bowlers.

The siren voices against this are mainly Australian, where even Prime Minister John Howard has called Murali a chucker. 'It's a huge coincidence that Murali's doosra is 14 degrees, and I find it extraordinary that they could have been 200 per cent out first time around,' said Shane Warne's coach, Terry Jenner.

Others are more pragmatic. Former Aussie skipper Ian Chappell says chucking decisions should be left to the umpires because (a) a blatant throw can be spotted with the naked eye and (b) a throw *has* to be blatant in order to achieve an advantage. He argues that too many restrictions on bowling actions will make batting too simple. 'If that's what the administrators want, then fine,' he said. 'But don't ask me to watch the resulting débâcle when Australia amass 1,350 runs to draw with India, who made 1,246.' Quite.

* Men's javelin world record holder (98.48 m)

— EASY WICKETS —

Taking a hat-trick is rare enough but in 1970 South African Trevor Goddard managed the (probably) unique feat of a hat-trick that wasn't. His first ball hit Duncan Fletcher's boot; Fletcher was given out, caught behind. The second clipped Errol Laughlin's pad; he went caught at slip. Determined not to surrender, next man Jackie du Preez took such a giant lunge down the wicket that it was nigh on impossible to give him lbw. It didn't matter: up went the finger. It was the perfect way for Goddard to end his last first-class match. The umpire must have forgotten to bring a leaving present.

— THE RUMBLE IN THE WACA —

English fans are fond of believing that Ashes Tests are the only ones that really matter, but try telling that to anyone who watched the match at the Western Australian Cricket Ground on 16 November 1981, when it was handbags at 12 o'clock between those punchy personalities Dennis 'The Stare' Lillee and 'Mighty' Javed Miandad. *Wisden Cricketers' Almanack* later described the contretemps as 'one of the most undignified incidents in Test history', which is another way of saying it was a belting good scrap.

Pakistan touring sides are rarely role models for corporate team-building but this particular year there was more than the usual degree of infighting. Several senior players made clear that they were unhappy with Miandad's appointment as skipper, and *Wisden* noted mildly that 'he did not appear to have the support of the whole team'. With Pakistan on 27–2 in the second innings of the first Test, still needing 543 and with two days to bat out, the pressure was on Miandad. All he needed was Lillee to turn up the heat.

Miandad had been building a decent stand with Mansoor Akhtar while Lillee, egged on by a well-lubricated crowd, had been serving up some short stuff. But the actual flashpoint was innocuous.

Miandad turned Lillee behind square and, in taking the easy single, collided with the bowler. Dennis later claimed that the two of them exchanged a few brief words of abuse; Javed said he'd been 'blocked and pushed out of the way' as he completed the run.

Then the fun really started. Lillee would claim that Miandad hit him from behind with his bat. Miandad reckoned Lillee had kicked him as he turned back to his mark. Either way, it was a feeding frenzy for the press. Pictures of umpire Tony Crafter holding back Lillee as Miandad wielded his bat head high dominated sports pages around the world.

The aftermath saw Lillee roundly blamed by Australian pundits. Former captain Bobby Simpson called it 'the most disgraceful thing I have seen on a cricket field'. Keith Miller called for Lillee to be suspended for the rest of the season, while Ian Chappell likened his actions to those of a 'spoiled, angry child'.

However, Chappell's brother, Greg – Australia's captain that day – rallied around his bowler, claiming that the confrontation was engineered as part of a plot to entrap Lillee. In those days there was a quaint old rule that Australian players disciplined themselves (a little like asking Ben Johnson to judge his own steroid abuse) and the dressing-room jury slapped a pathetically low fine of Aus$200 on Lillee. Both umpires immediately complained about this leniency, and the Australian Board replaced the punishment with a two-match suspension and Aus$120 fine. Curiously, this meant that Lillee had to miss just two uninspiring ODIs. He was back for the second Test, dismissed Miandad twice and helped Australia to a ten-wicket win.

The protagonists harrumphed a lot about the clash afterwards, and each maintained he was innocent. They eventually agreed to forgive and are back on speaking terms. But will they forget? Doubtful.

— ODI HIGHEST TEAM SCORES —

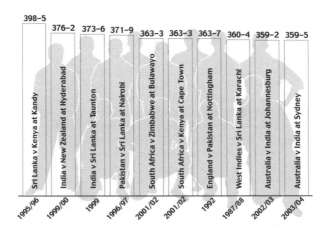

Score	Match	Year
398–5	Sri Lanka v Kenya at Kandy	1995/96
376–2	India v New Zealand at Hyderabad	1999/00
373–6	India v Sri Lanka at Taunton	1999
371–9	Pakistan v Sri Lanka at Nairobi	1996/97
363–3	South Africa v Zimbabwe at Bulawayo	2001/02
363–3	South Africa v Kenya at Cape Town	2001/02
363–7	England v Pakistan at Nottingham	1992
360–4	West Indies v Sri Lanka at Karachi	1987/88
359–2	Australia v India at Johannesburg	2002/03
359–5	Australia v India at Sydney	2003/04

— ODI LOWEST TEAM SCORES —

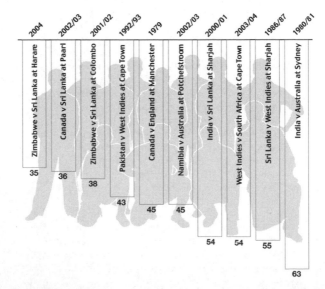

Year	Match	Score
2004	Zimbabwe v Sri Lanka at Harare	35
2002/03	Canada v Sri Lanka at Paarl	36
2001/02	Zimbabwe v Sri Lanka at Colombo	38
1992/93	Pakistan v West Indies at Cape Town	43
1979	Canada v England at Manchester	45
2002/03	Namibia v Australia at Potchefstroom	45
2000/01	India v Sri Lanka at Sharjah	54
2003/04	West Indies v South Africa at Cape Town	54
1986/87	Sri Lanka v West Indies at Sharjah	55
1980/81	India v Australia at Sydney	63

— TON MACHINE —

Stand-in Aussie captain Adam Gilchrist emerged from the victorious 2004 tour of India with 11 Test 100s to his name – just one short of the all-time record for wicket-keepers, held by Zimbabwe's Andy Flower. Gilchrist also boasts one of cricket's more unusual claims to fame in that each one of those tons was scored on a different ground. His tally reads as follows:

AUSTRALIA	Brisbane, Hobart, Perth and Sydney
SOUTH AFRICA	Cape Town and Jo'burg
WEST INDIES	Port of Spain
ENGLAND	Edgbaston
SRI LANKA	Kandy

— TENDULKAR, INC —

Eastern religions aren't big on saints, but if they were then Sachin Tendulkar would be a living one. It's hard to think of anyone else, in any walk of life, who can bring an entire nation to a standstill just by strolling out to work. How did India ever get by without him?

Tendulkar was the first to score 50 100s in international cricket, but it's not just his career record (by 2004, almost 23,000 runs in Tests and ODIs at an overall average of 50.52) that has elevated him to India's pantheon of sporting gods. Tendulkar is bright, good-looking and very, very rich. He's had a car named after him (also known as the Fiat Palio S10), featured in a musical *(I Am Sachin Tendulkar)*, opened two eateries in Mumbai (unsurprisingly called Tendulkar's and Sachin's) and has launched a mesmerising range of sportswear. He has even contributed to a school textbook used by primary-school pupils in Delhi, who discover on reading it that he used to collect coins as a child. No change there, you might say.

Not everything Sachin touches turns to gold, though. He was a distinctly average Test captain (played 25, won 4, lost 9, drawn 12) and became frustrated with players too easily. Fast bowler Javagal Srinath hinted as much when he wrote in one newspaper, 'He could bowl leg spin, he could swing the ball and of course he could bat like Tendulkar. And he expected the same standards from everyone.'

— A QUICK RÉSUMÉ —

Truly great Test fast bowlers work best hunting in pairs. Here are England's top five in order of debut.

LARWOOD AND VOCE

The shock troops of the 1932/3 'bodyline' series. Given their fearsome reputation, it seems strange that this Nottinghamshire pair played just the one series together – especially since it produced a combined total of 41 wickets over the four matches they played in tandem. Voce missed the fourth Test although his absence had little effect on Larwood, who bagged another seven scalps. Their AST (Average Strikes per Test) is 10.25.

TRUEMAN AND STATHAM

Brought together in their 20s, this pair were the perfect combination: Trueman fast, aggressive and dogged; Statham unerringly accurate and deceptively quick. Together they took 284 wickets in 35 Tests – England's greatest-ever new ball partnership – recording an AST of 8.1. (The toppest of all top facts about Trueman is that, alongside Alan Donald, he holds the record for playing the greatest number of Tests without ever emerging wicketless. Both men managed 67.)

WILLIS AND BOTHAM

Few batsman ever regarded themselves as 'in' against these two. The giant Willis could deliver raw pace with a steepling bounce, while Botham was genuinely quick with a boomerang-style swing in the right conditions. At their peak, between 1978 and 1982, they took 172 wickets in 24 Tests to produce an AST of 7.1.

CADDICK AND GOUGH

Caddick, particularly, seems to have missed out on the plaudits, perhaps because a dip in form in 2002 allowed him to be too easily edged out by rising stars. Gough was always a favourite with the Barmy Army, his fast in-swinging yorker as lethal on its day as anything conjured up by Waqar Younis. The pairing came into its own in 1999, just as Duncan Fletcher took the helm as England coach, and took 190 wickets in 25 successive Tests, playing a major part in helping England win four series on the bounce. Their AST score is 7.6.

HARMISON AND JONES

There have been many false dawns for genuinely quick England bowling partnerships, but this isn't one of them. Both men are superb athletes and offer contrasting styles: Harmison with his extraordinary lift; Jones an old-ball specialist who likes to 'skid' the ball into a batsman's body. Either way, the ball arrives at anything up to 95mph, making them comfortably the fastest, most hostile pair ever to take the field in an England cap. During five Tests together in 2004, they took 46 wickets, bringing their AST rating up to 9.2.

— DEAD WRONG —

Cricket supporters must occasionally wonder whether their team's slip fielders have died in action – or, rather, inaction. Few players, though, have actually been presented with a wreath by their club.

However, Carlisle CC seems distinctly trigger-happy when shuffling players off on that long walk to the pavilion in the sky. When Carlisle's committee heard that a veteran – Leonard Brunton, affectionately known as 'Bunt' – had passed away, they paid their respects in exemplary fashion. Players held a minute's silence, the ground flag was flown at half mast and an official representative, Albert Clapperton, was despatched to present the family with a wreath.

After knocking on the door, it quickly became apparent that 66-year-old Mr Brunton was the opposite of dead. Someone had misread a local paper obituary. Fortunately, Bunt took it all in good heart. 'It was pretty weird,' he said, 'but I was really touched.'

— LUNCHBOX POLICE —

Cricket followers are a naturally conservative lot, which is why topless cricket is probably still some way off. Even in Australia – a country that defines itself on suspicion of protocol – there is a dogged determination to uphold standards. Why else would the South Australian Cricket Association rigorously enforce its dress code in the Adelaide Oval members' enclosure, banning gear such as board shorts, 'revealing' tops, thongs, jeans with designer tears and tracksuit bottoms?

Such action might get a nod of approval from retired colonels (though not *all* retired colonels) but tinkering with freedom of choice is a dangerous business in the cash-hungry world of modern cricket. What if Levi sponsored a future ICC Champions' Trophy? Would *their* ripped jeans be banned by SACA? And what about the putative 'Adidas Ashes'? Which Adelaide Oval official, exactly, is going to kick out spectators arriving in Adidas jogging pants?

If this all seems far-fetched, rest assured, it isn't. Had you told an English cricket supporter arriving for a game in the 1970s that his lunchbox – and we're talking lunchbox in the traditional rather than colloquial sense – was to be inspected for illegal crisps, nuts and fizzy drinks, he'd have given you an earful. Yet lunchbox crime is now a fact of life at English cricket grounds, as spectators attending 2004 ICC Champions' Trophy matches well know. On receiving their tickets by post, they discovered a warning from tournament director David Clarke, who began by stressing the important role of sponsors and then added: 'I would therefore like to take this opportunity to bring to your attention that non-alcoholic beverages (including water and soft drinks) not produced by Pepsi and crisps and snacks not produced by Walkers will not be permitted into the venue for matches during the tournament.'

Leaving aside that tortuous hat-trick of negatives, Clarke's words caused apoplexy among many ticket-holders. The best response came from Richard Bonnor-Morris, of London, who in a letter to *The Times* wrote, 'The ICC have taken it on themselves to restrict the contents of my lunchbox. Firstly, I question the ICC's right to dictate which water I drink at any time. Secondly, I dread to think of the length of time I shall have to wait while everyone's bags are searched to ensure no contraband beverage is found.' He concluded, 'I for one will be attending the final in a Coca-Cola-can outfit, which I assume is permitted, as it is neither a beverage nor a snack.'

The ICC and ECB's motives were apparently to prevent 'ambush marketing', such as that deployed by, oh yes, Pepsi, during the 1996 World Cup in India. On that occasion, Coca-Cola were the official sponsors and Pepsi flew blimps bearing its logo near some of the grounds.

— BET ON MILLER —

There have been a few playboy cricketers, but none quite match the debonair, devil-may-care Australian all-rounder Keith Miller. His experience as a wartime fighter pilot and dedicated racing punter gave him a nonchalance about life – and cricket – that foolish opponents sometimes mistook for indifference. It was a view Miller often encouraged as captain of New South Wales. Fielders approaching him for instructions at the start of an innings would be told loudly and dismissively, 'Just scatter.'

This was pure showboating. Miller was a shrewd and careful tactician who liked to work things out in advance, often communicating on the field with a subtle nod of the head or wave of his hand. Richie Benaud regarded him as the best captain Australia never had, although he could be a nightmare to those he served; Ian Johnson – hardly a great Aussie skipper himself – once said of Miller, 'He can't bat, he can't bowl, he can't field and he gives me the shits.' Miller's record proved otherwise: he struck 14,183 runs (average 48.90) and took 497 wickets (at 22.26) during his first-class career, and in 55 Tests he amassed 2,958 runs (at 36.97) with 170 wickets (at 22.97).

It's easy to have some sympathy with Johnson. By the 1956 Ashes series in England, Miller – then close to international retirement – was giving off distinctly negative vibes. Age had caught up with him and, like many of his team-mates, he was perplexed by Jim Laker's off-spin. So it was that, late in the series, as Laker again wreaked havoc, Johnson tried manfully to rally the troops with a dressing-room pep talk. 'With guts and determination,' he cried, 'we can still save this match.' Miller barely glanced up from the racing pages. 'Betcha six to four we can't,' he said.

— NERVOUS NINETY-NINERS —

Nothing, but nothing, in cricket is as gut-wrenchingly dreadful as being out on 99. Mike Atherton, Geoff Boycott and Mike Smith all qualify on two counts for this England 'Nearly Men' XI. As well as the games listed below, Atherton just missed out against Australia, at Lord's in 1993; Boycott was left stranded on 99 despite carrying his bat in the 1979 first Test against Australia at the WACA; and Smith was a run short at Lord's against the 1960 South Africa team.

NAME	VENUE	OPPONENTS	YEAR
ME Trescothick	Sardar Patel Stadium	India	2001
AJ Tudor	Edgbaston	New Zealand	1999
MA Atherton	Headingley	South Africa	1994
MD Moxon	Eden Park	New Zealand	1988
GA Gooch	MCG	Australia	1980
G Boycott	Queen's Park	West Indies	1974
D Amiss	National Stadium	Pakistan	1973
ER Dexter	BCG	Australia	1962
MJ K Smith	Gadaffi Stadium	Pakistan	1961
E Paynter	Lord's	Australia	1938
H Sutcliffe	Newlands	South Africa	1927

— SO NEAR, SO BAD —

Cricket statisticians, like weathermen, take great pride in casually announcing (usually in bored tones) that the amazing events you've just witnessed are, actually, not very remarkable. Had you been at Mumbai in 2004 for the final India vs Australia Test, you might have felt safe in putting forward the 108 target set by India as the lowest a chasing Test side has ever failed to reach. Indian supporters will gleefully recall that Australia shouldered arms for 93.

Sadly, your claim would have been swatted faster than a burger on Shane Warne's barbie. In 1882, Australia skittled England for 77, having set them just 85 to win, and in the 1999/2000 series between the West Indies and Zimbabwe, the African tourists surrendered for an abject 63, falling 37 short of victory. Trivia is one thing, but beware statisticians bearing scorebooks.

— THE 'DIRTY DOZEN' —

In 1982, after 12 years in the sporting wilderness, South African cricket lovers were desperate to watch their latest generation of players face some first-class international opposition. With apartheid still in place, an official Test was out of the question, but Yorkshire and England opener Geoff Boycott signed a business deal to organise an unofficial England tour. His squad – largely cobbled together from players nearing the end of their careers – became known as the 'Dirty Dozen'. The original selection was:

Graham Gooch (captain)
Geoffrey Boycott
Dennis Amiss
Wayne Larkins
John Emburey
Alan Knott
Peter Willey
Mike Hendrick
Chris Old
John Lever
Les Taylor
Derek Underwood

These players were roundly accused of sacrificing personal morality for a bumper pay day. They contended that sport had nothing to do with politics – and it's fair to say that, at the time, there was little sign of Pretoria's racist regime *ever* capitulating to the international ban. Only now is it clear that isolation from sports such as cricket played a crucial part in forcing the South Africans' hand.

As it turned out, the Dirty Dozen's tour was little more than a series of glorified four-day exhibition games, dominated by the home side. It meant very little in cricketing terms, because any England team without Ian Botham (then at his absolute peak) was always going to be hopelessly devalued. The tour also ended the Test careers of Boycott, Knott, Old, Hendrick and Underwood.

— NO GENTLEMAN, JIM —

Previous items have alluded to 'gentlemen' and 'players' in the context of early cricket matches, and today's supporter can certainly be forgiven for asking, 'What's *that* all about?' Basically, the English establishment gave a collective shudder at the thought of plebeians being paid to play cricket, so they introduced a distinction by which professional players became 'Players' and amateur players became 'Gentlemen'. (Don't laugh, Australian readers!)

Strangely, England's first captain in the first official Test match – against the Aussies in Melbourne at the start of the 1876/7 tour – was James Lillywhite. He was demonstrably a professional, since the entire team was being paid through privately raised funds. Home captains were, however, always Gentlemen, and after the MCC assumed responsibility for overseas tours at the start of the 20th century, they always threw in a couple of proper Gents. One of these was invariably made captain.

The first cracks in this tradition appeared in 1953, when Len Hutton got the England skipper's berth for an Ashes tour, mainly because there was absolutely no one else. Curiously, he wasn't even captain of his county – Yorkshire – at the time, because they still wanted an amateur in charge. The distinction was finally abolished in July 1962, with the last Gentleman-vs-Players match – the 137th in a sequence stretching back to 1806 – taking place at Lord's, with Ted Dexter and Fred Trueman serving as captains. (Have a guess who was the Gentleman and who the Player.) The three-day match was drawn, leaving the Players with a final tally of 68 victories to the Gentlemen's 41.

— RINGER ALERT —

The Gentlemen weren't always so gentlemanly in their pursuit of victory. In the game held in 1825, for instance, they managed to persuade the Players to let them field 16 men. Not only that but one of them was a ringer, the Players' very own W Matthews, who took the opportunity to clean-bowl six of his team-mates and see off a seventh, caught and bowled. The Gents chortled their way to a 72-run victory.

— BITTER SWEET —

Considering the way his extraordinary skills have brightened venues around the world, the autumn of Brian Lara's career has been uncharacteristically gloomy. The ignominy of England's 2004 'blackwash' on the back of a 3–0 home series defeat happened on his watch, and Lara's recent results as captain – albeit leading a poor team – have been little short of dire. His skipper's record to September 2004 showed that he'd won 23 out of 40 Tests, but only three of his last 25. Moreover, his personal end-of-term report must have read something like, 'Batting genius, could do better.'

West Indian fans will point to the outstanding 400 he posted against England in 2004, although that innings – on an absolute jewel of an Antiguan wicket – is the exception that proves the rule. Set it aside and you discover the Windies skipper averaged just 26 in the seven other Tests he played against Michael Vaughan's side. He also failed to score a 100 in what will almost certainly be his last series in England. By Lara's standards, that's a damning statistic: the first time in six series against England that he has failed to hit a century off their bowlers.

Perhaps on a damp and bleak late-September evening at The Oval, the cricketing gods decided it was time to give Lara a break. With his side stumbling towards defeat in the ICC Champions' Trophy final at 147–8, Courtney Browne and Ian Bradshaw conjured up a West Indian record ninth-wicket stand of 71 to take their side to victory by two wickets with seven balls to spare. That gutsy performance ensured that one of the world's all-time great batsmen got a fitting send-off from the English game. Really, you couldn't make it up.

— TIMED OUT —

One of the most irksome souvenirs you'll ever see is
a tea towel imprinted with 'the laws of cricket as
explained to a foreigner'. You know the one: 'You
have two sides, one out in the field and one in. Each
man that's in the side that's in goes out, and when
he's out, he comes in and the next man goes in until
he's out.' Yet there are some aspects of cricket that
must be genuinely baffling to the casual observer:
those long, dog-day afternoons when the run rate
slows, the bowlers get bored, long on becomes nod
off and any hope of a result is a cruelly distant dream.
This scenario pretty much applies to the first Test
between New Zealand and South Africa at Auckland
in March 1999, when the Kiwis' last man, Geoff
Allott, faced 77 balls, occupied the crease for 101
minutes and was finally caught Pollock, bowled Kallis,
for nought.

In fairness, Allott didn't have a whole bundle of
options. New Zealand were battling to save the
follow-on at 320–9, and as South Africa had declared
on 621–5 it was hardly his cue for a swashbuckling
display of batsmanship. He was also denied the
chance to take some easy singles, deferring to the
cautious approach of Chris Harris at the other end.
In the event, their 32-run partnership was 70 short
of the follow-on target, but it did help them to secure
a draw.

Afterwards, the ebullient Allott relished his place in
Test history, firstly as the Kiwi who'd taken longest
to open his account (beating John Wright's 66 minutes)
and secondly as the new holder of Godfrey Evans' all-
comers record for the longest period on nought (64
balls and 97 minutes, for England against South Africa
in 1947). Even so, he can't quite match the claim to
fame of fellow New Zealander Martin Snedden, who
in 1990 batted on each of the first three days of the
rain-affected first Test at Trent Bridge before being
caught Gooch, bowled DeFreitas, for a big fat zero.

Finally, a word for two undisputed English masters of the forward defensive: Trevor Bailey and Chris Tavaré. Bailey was a world-class fast-medium bowler whose batting skills extracted England from a deep hole on many occasions. His most stubborn deployment of the 'Bailey Block' came during the first Ashes Test at Brisbane in December 1958, when he batted for a total of 357 minutes to score the slowest half-century in the history of first-class cricket, at an average speed of one run every seven minutes.

Tavaré, meanwhile, had a knack of infuriating every bowling attack he faced – particularly that of the Australians – by combining a technically superb defence with a propensity to jog off to square leg between balls. His greatest snub to aggressive batsmanship came during the 1982 first Test between Australia and England at Perth when, in his first innings, he was stuck on 66 for an astonishing 90 minutes. In the second, he took 63 minutes to score his first run and went on to make 9 from 82 balls (equivalent to 0.109 per ball, since you ask). For years it was a standard gag in panto for the Sleeping Beauty to enquire drowsily of her prince, 'Is Tavaré off the mark yet?'

— SO CLOSE —

Donald Bradman needed just four runs in the 1948 Ashes Test at The Oval to leave Test cricket with an average of 100 from 80 innings. It was only one good blow, but it never came, and he retired on 99.94. Whisper it quietly (especially to Australians), but there was a batsman of that era who left Test cricket with better figures than Bradman: the West Indies opener Andy Ganteaume.

Ganteaume finished with an average of 112 thanks to his sole Test-match innings of 112 against England at Port of Spain in 1948. He later claimed he was dropped to make way for 'establishment' players, and he may well have a point. It's hard to see how the Windies' selectors could have been any crueller.

— PC TIPS —

In the heat of battle, players occasionally say the wrong thing. In Mark Barlow's case, it proved wrong enough to get him an eight-week ban and a six-point penalty for his team – Derbyshire-based Cutthorpe Seconds – during a match at Newark, Nottinghamshire.

During a break in proceedings, Barlow suggested to team-mates that Kate Lowe, a former England international who was at the crease, should 'go home and get her husband's tea'. Hardly original, but it was enough to register a complaint to the Bassetlaw League Disciplinary Committee.

Barlow apologised to Lowe at the hearing, admitting that his words 'might be slightly sexist'. But, he added, 'It's PC gone bananas. I'm amazed it has gone so far. What happens on the pitch should stay on the pitch. It's too harsh. I apologised and shook her hand, but she got up on her high horse and got a bee in her bonnet.' Lucky he wasn't done for cliché abuse as well.

— MENACING DENNIS —

The record for most Test wickets in a calendar year is held by Australia's Dennis Lillee, who took 85 in 1981. Ian Botham held the English record (66 in 1978) until 2004, when Steve Harmison seized the crown during the 2004/05 tour of South Africa (see page 176).

— ISLE BE DARNED —

In these days of Euro-scepticism, it's refreshing to note that there is a far-flung EU isle that is forever England. Unlikely as it sounds, the remote Croatian territory of Vis, in the Adriatic, has a fanatical cricket following that stages impromptu games played on a daily basis. The enthusiasm of the island's William Hoste Cricket Club recently won it a £7,000 coaching grant from the European Cricket Council.

For readers unfamiliar with Napoleonic sea battles, Captain William Hoste was one of the Royal Navy's greatest heroes, a commander who, though outnumbered three to one by enemy ships, routed the French fleet off Vis in 1811. As the Gallic foe fled his cannon, Hoste's flagship raised the signal 'Remember Nelson' (who had fallen at Trafalgar six years previously). Victory, according to the Cap'n, was never in doubt; he knew his men had gleaned the batting basics of a good forward-defensive shot. The French never had a prayer.

There is only slight poetic licence in this account. Hoste had indeed been naval commander of the Vis Adriatic station for three years prior to his French engagement, and in a letter home he described the sun-kissed island as a perfect venue for England's summer game. 'We have established a cricket club and when we anchor for a few hours it passes away the time quite wonderfully,' he wrote. The letter also praised the natives for the way they joined in matches.

Hoste's hope that cricket would be a lasting British legacy proved unfounded until 2001, when a Vis wine grower called Oliver Roki read his biography. Mr Roki read up on the Laws of the game and within a few months the William Hoste CC was formed. 'People here have taken to the game with a passion I find incredible,' said Roki. 'Even local fishermen come ashore, leaving their boats for hours at a time to play a game. We are kings of improvisation. We play it everywhere: among the palm trees, on small uninhabited off-shore islands – everywhere.'

— STRAIGHT TALK —

Former Aussie Test batsman and TV commentator Dean Jones was in typically cautious mode when asked his views about cricket in Zimbabwe. 'We just have to be careful what we say about [Premier Robert] Mugabe,' said Jones. 'But I'm just there to watch the cricket, and I don't give a rat's arse what he does about his country.'

— CRUEL GAME —

Durham shelled out spondulicks by the thousand to sign five overseas players for 2004: Shoaib Akhtar, Andy Blignaut, Marcus North, Reon King and the much-vaunted Aussie pace prodigy Shaun Tait. It didn't help much; the county bagged a mere £10,000 in prize money, and among Tait's less impressive returns was this one: 18–0–176–0.

— CHIN UP —

Everyone's allowed a grumpy day at the office once in a while, but if you're a cricket commentator, you're not supposed to burden the public with your personal woes. So PC users logged on to *The Guardian*'s internet coverage of a 2003 World Cup tie between India and New Zealand were very surprised to read the opening lines of Scott Murray's report, which consisted of a diatribe in capital letters on the dour nature of his workaday world.

'What sort of life is this, and what the hell am I doing boarding a train for Moorgate at 6:30 in the morning?' bemoaned Murray. 'I know cricket's good and all that, but I've got out of the wrong side of bed this morning, and in any case it's not as if I'll write a cracking match report and then get rewarded by being sent on a wonderful assignment around the world, because I'll be very surprised if any of my bosses will read any of this.'

Somewhat bashfully, Murray apologised to readers for not delivering 'the sort of quality editorial copy you expect from *The Guardian*.' But he added, 'Look at the facts. I'm adrift in the middle of one of the worst cities in the world, sitting in front of the same computer screen I face day after interminable day.' *The Guardian* was – publicly at least – relaxed about Murray's comments. 'It is very much in keeping with the spirit and tone of our cricket coverage,' said a spokesman.

— MAIDEN TOUR —

The first women's Ashes Test was played at the Exhibition Ground (long demolished) in Brisbane between 28 and 31 December 1934. England bowled out their hosts for 47, won the match by nine wickets, took the three-match series 3–0 and later travelled on to New Zealand, where they won the inaugural Test by an innings and 337 runs. It was just as well they enjoyed themselves: members of the tour party were expected to pay their own expenses, estimated at around £80 per head.

— YOUNG GUNS —

In the modern game, only four players have scored Test centuries for England before reaching the age of 22: Denis Compton (the youngest ever, aged 20), David Gower, Len Hutton and Peter May. To this elite band you can add in brackets the name of Michael Atherton, whose innings of 151 against New Zealand at Trent Bridge in 1990 came less than 12 weeks after his 22nd birthday.

— FILTHY RICH —

Cricketers may still be the poor relations of international sport when compared to golfers, Formula One drivers, tennis stars and soccer players, but the gap is steadily closing – especially for winners. England's run of seven consecutive Test wins in summer 2004 earned the side $1.4 million (£800,000), and victory in the Champions' Trophy final would have pushed this above $2 million (£1.1 million).

— A WOMAN'S TOUCH —

There must have been mutterings in the Long Room, but in May 2003 the England women's cricket captain Clare Connor became the first woman in Britain to provide live TV commentary for a Test match. She made her debut for Channel 4 at Lord's during the first Test against Zimbabwe.

— CRUEL STATS —

Statistics can be so unforgiving at times. Just 24 hours after securing his 400th Test wicket, Indian spinner Anil Kumble discovered he had the dubious distinction of conceding 100 runs in an innings on 32 occasions. That's more than any other bowler apart from the mercurial Muttiah Muralitharan, who has managed it 42 times. Despite this, both men would surely walk into any international squad in the world.

As for the Englishman in third position – who conceded 100 runs in each of 31 Tests – it's hard to see how any selection panel would cross out the name of IT Botham.

— WIND ASSISTED —

'Rain stopped play' is a familiar refrain in world cricket. 'Wind stopped play' is a rather more unusual occurrence. It did happen, briefly, during Australia's 1993/4 tour of South Africa as the visitors took on Orange Free State at Bloemfontein. Aussie fast bowler Merv Hughes – known as something of a trencherman – must have had an extra helping of beans for breakfast because just as he accelerated to the crease, he broke wind. That's putting it mildly. It was one rip-snorting delivery.

South African captain Hansie Cronje, who was on strike, instantly dissolved in a fit of giggles. Hughes joined in the ribaldry and within seconds every player on the pitch was in hysterics. It took a full three minutes for the umpires to restore order and for Hughes to complete his over. Cronje had no cause for complaint; he went on to score a career-best 251.

— SERIAL WINNERS —

The record for most Test series without defeat is held by the great West Indies side that came together in the late 1970s. They notched up an incredible 29 wins between 1980 and 1995, when Australia finally turned them over. England are in second place – unbeaten in 14 series between 1951 and 1958 – but by the end of 2004 the Aussies looked well placed to overtake.

— GOOD START —

Sometimes you just know it's going to be your day. On 26 November 1999, Sri Lanka's Nuwan Zoysa opened the bowling on the first day of the second Test against Zimbabwe at Harare and got a hat-trick off his first three balls. The unfortunate victims were Trevor Gripper, Murray Goodwin and Neil Johnson. Zimbabwe were skittled for 174 in their first innings, and Sri Lanka won the game by six wickets.

— THERE'S A THING —

Psychologists tell us that coincidences are, you know, just a coincidence. Even so, the result of the 100th-anniversary Test match between Australia and England, played at the Melbourne Cricket Ground on 12, 13, 14, 16 and 17 March 1977, stretched credulity just a little. The result was that Australia won by 45 runs – precisely the same as their winning margin at the MCG in the inaugural Ashes match on 15, 16, 17 and 19 March 1877. Strictly speaking, this first game wasn't a Test match, because the phrase wasn't coined until 16 September 1884, when it first appeared in the *Melbourne Argus*.

— BOXING CLEVER —

Fame works in mysterious ways. After his outstanding 2004 season, Andrew Flintoff prepared for England's South African tour by spending a month in a Salford sweatbox called Oliver's Gym, training HQ for some of Britain's most promising young boxers.

The idea went down well with sports editors, and pictures of the boy wonder in boxing gloves beneath headlines like 'Freddie Packs A Punch' got a good show. However, the effect on Flintoff's public profile is less clear. On his way home one night, he stopped at a local video store only to realise he'd forgotten his membership card. 'Don't worry,' said the assistant, 'I know who you are. You're that boxer.'

— TEST WINNING STREAKS —

Total	Country	Start	Finish
16	Australia	Harare, 1999	Mumbai, 2001
11	West Indies	Bridgetown, 1984	Adelaide, 1984
9	South Africa	Durban, 2002	Dhaka, 2003
9	Sri Lanka	Colombo, 2001	Lahore, 2002
8	Australia	Sydney, 1920	Leeds, 1921
8	England	Lord's 2004	Port Elizabeth, 2004

— RUN FEST —

No two teams have ever managed to score 600 apiece in a single innings in the same match, but this feat was almost achieved in the fifth Test of England's 1993/4 tour to the West Indies at St John's, Antigua. The Windies made 593–5, declared (Lara 375), while England were all out for an identical score (Smith 175, Atherton 135). On another occasion, the West Indies and Pakistan scored a total of 1,236 between them at Bridgetown, Barbados, during the 1957/8 series, but that was divided 579–657, respectively.

— AUSSIE-DODGERS —

Since Australia are the pace-setters for international cricket, it follows that individual players must be partly judged on their records against Aussie opponents. This is just about the only question mark left over Andrew Flintoff's ability. Before the 2005 Ashes series, he held the England record for playing the most Tests (40), without ever playing Australia. At the time of writing, the South Africa–MCC series should add another five.

While this comfortably beats England's previous best Aussie-dodger (Nick Knight, on 17), it will never rival the undisputed world champion, New Zealand all-rounder John Reid, who played his entire career (58 Tests) without ever seeing a baggy green cap. (In fairness, that's because the countries didn't play each other in an official series between 1946 and 1973.)

— TIRESOME BOWLING —

When England's Fred Trueman became the first bowler in Test history to reach the 300-wicket mark (The Oval, 1964, vs Australia), he was asked by one reporter if anyone would ever break his record. 'Aye,' replied the no-nonsense Yorkshireman, 'but whoever does will be bloody tired.'

Trueman's aura of greatness was not merely the result of his outstanding record (307 wickets at an average of 21.57). He was no mean exponent of psychological warfare and enjoyed wandering into opposition dressing rooms to inform rookie opponents helpfully that a few balls would be bouncing around their ears. 'Can you hook, son?' Trueman would enquire. ''Cause you'll get the chance today.'

— BODY BLOWS —

The traditional fast bowler's tactic for softening up new batsman is brutally simple: give 'em a bit of 'chin music' (ie a bouncer) or, better still, get a ball to actually hit them. All Test batsman have taken painful blows in their time, but perhaps the most stalwart display of defiance – certainly by an Englishman – was the pulverising Brian Close took when he was recalled at the age of 45 to face the 1976 West Indies tourists.

Subjected to a barrage of short-pitched bowling from Holding, Roberts and Daniels, Close's upper body erupted into a mass of bruises, none of which he deigned to rub (at least, not publicly). Seemingly impervious to pain, he would laconically ask players who flinched at such treatment, 'How can the ball hurt you? It's only on you for a second.'

Close's talent as an all-rounder was never equal to his courage, but he still holds the record as England's youngest debutant, against New Zealand in 1949, when he was just 18. Supporters remember his finest hour as the Lord's Test against West Indies in 1963, when he took apart the tourists' pace attack, striding menacingly down the wicket in a thrilling display of attacking cricket. That 70 was his highest Test score, and it took England to within six runs of victory before time ran out.

— DUCK'S REVENGE —

Superstitions are rife in cricket dressing rooms, and one particular old favourite is that you should never eat duck on the eve of a game.

At the end of the fourth day of the 1982 Lord's Test against Pakistan, the position was tense with England needing a single run to avoid the follow on. Robin Jackman, who'd earlier bowled well for his four wickets, was last man in. He was not renowned for his batting prowess.

To lighten things up, Jackman, David Gower and Allan Lamb went out for a meal at a good French restaurant. Guess what? They all ordered duck. The next day, Jackman was immediately out, lbw, to Imran Khan, and both Gower (caught) and Lamb (lbw) followed suit. They should have had a nice, well-done steak instead. England lost by ten wickets.

— B&B STAYERS —

'Checking in for bed and breakfast' is one of those fine, old cricketing clichés that do so much to mystify the game for the general public. It refers to an incoming batsman who, late in the day, is under orders to block every ball and keep his wicket intact for the following morning's session.

HIGHEST TEST SCORES FOR EACH BATTING POSITION — AS AT DECEMBER 2004 —

Position	Player	Country	Opponent	Score	Date	Venue
1/2	ML Hayden	Aus	Zim	380	09/10/2003	WACA
3	BC Lara	WI	Eng	400	10/04/2004	Antigua Rec
4	Inzamam-ul-Haq	Pak	NZ	329	01/05/2002	Gadaffi Stad
5	DG Bradman	Aus	Eng	304	20/07/1934	Headingley
6	KD Walters	Aus	NZ	250	18/02/1977	Jade Stadium
7	DG Bradman	Aus	Eng	270	01/01/1937	MCG
8	Wasim Akram	Pak	Zim	257	17/10/1996	Sheikhupura Stadium
9	IDS Smith	NZ	Ind	173	22/02/1990	Eden Park
10	WW Read	Eng	Aus	117	11/08/1884	The Oval
11	Zaheer Khan	Ind	Bangladesh	75	10/12/2004	Bangabandhu Stad

— WILCO ROGER —

Fast bowlers are a temperamental lot who don't always embrace constructive criticism, so when Pakistan coach and former England batsman Bob Woolmer suggested that Shoaib Akhtar should cut down his run-up (currently well over 40 yards) there was always going to be fireworks.

Woolmer was livid at Pakistan's over rate during their embarrassing 491-run defeat in the December 2004 Perth Test, describing it as 'ridiculous and very poor'. The other big problem was that, having reduced Australia to 5 for 78 in their first innings, Pakistan could not maintain pressure because Akhtar's lengthy sprints confined him to five-over spells.

Woolmer isn't the first Pakistan coach to tackle the world's fastest bowler on this thorny question, but Shoaib is not for turning – at least, not until he's walked back the full 40. 'I'll ask you a question,' he challenged a *Sydney Morning Herald* journalist. 'Can a plane take off without a run-up? No. So I've got to take the run. It's how I generate my pace, and everything flows into the right action. I'm not going to cut down.' The sluggish over rate would be improved, he said, by 'going back to my run-up quickly'.

It's hard for Pakistan supporters to be too critical of Akhtar, especially as he was by far their best player at Perth, taking six wickets in the match. Even so, old hands despair at his stubbornness. 'I used to bowl all day at his age,' sighed Imran Khan. 'He sprints such a long way that he could easily cut it down without losing any pace.'

— ENGLAND VS EUROPE —

A total of 42 batsmen passed the magic 1,000-run mark during the 2004 English county season. Of these, 30 were qualified to play for England. The worrying thing for the selectors, though, is that 41 EU-qualified and 62 foreign players appeared in county line-ups. Of the foreigners, more than half were Australian. Nothing like a recce of the battlefield – an Ashes 2005 battlefield, that is – before hostilities commence!

— MIND GAMES —

You can train like a Spartan, sweat blood in the nets and practise catching until your pinkies tingle, but Test matches are mostly fought in the mind. Simply being gifted and fit doesn't bag a seat at cricket's High Table, and even those who *have* proved themselves are often dogged by puzzling under-performances. From the players' point of view, cricket statisticians are depressingly good at spotting this sort of thing.

Take Somerset's Marcus Trescothick, whose overall record as an England opener makes him both literally and figuratively the first name on the team sheet. With 861 Test runs in 2002, 1,003 in 2003 and over 900 in 2004 he is also admirably consistent. But a harder look at his record home and away reveals a strange truth. As they say in the West Country, Trescothick travels worse than a brown dog in a thunderstorm. Something like that, anyway.

The following table illustrates his problem going into the 2004/5 South Africa series. It includes all Tests up to his second innings at Durban, when, perhaps stung by accusations of 'tour gips', he posted an imperious 132 – his top score on foreign territory. Even so, Trescothick – an enthusiastic exponent of yoga – could do with meditating hard on the following analysis of his home and away form:

	HOME TESTS	TOURING TESTS
PLAYED	28	28
SCORED	2,373	1,806
TOP SCORE	219	132
HALF CENTURIES	15	9
CENTURIES	6	3
AVERAGE	53.9	34.7

Before Trescothick fans start writing rude letters, it should be mentioned that a Test average of 34.7 is hardly the stuff of failure. Trescothick is unquestionably world class, and his position as England's top run scorer in 2003 – in both Tests and ODIs (see below) – is quite enough to see off the critics. As for Ricky Ponting, presumably he'd just like to bottle 2003.

LEADING TEST RUN SCORERS IN 2003

PLAYER/COUNTRY	MATCHES/ INNINGS	TOTAL RUNS	NOT OUT	AVERAGE
RT Ponting/Aus	11/18	1503	3	100.20
BC Lara/WI	10/19	1344	1	74.67
ML Hayden/Aus	12/21	1312	4	77.18
GC Smith/SA	12/19	1198	0	63.05
HH Gibbs/SA	12/19	1156	1	64.22
ME Trescothick /Eng	13/24	1003	3	47.76
MA Butcher/Eng	13/23	979	1	44.50
MP Vaughan/Eng	13/24	958	1	41.65
G Kirsten/SA	8/13	889	1	74.08
ST Waugh/Aus	12/15	876	4	79.64
JL Langer/Aus	12/21	824	1	41.20

LEADING ODI RUN SCORERS IN 2003

PLAYER/COUNTRY	MATCHES/ INNINGS	TOTAL RUNS	NOT OUT	AVERAGE
Yousuf Youhana/Pak	33/31	1168	4	43.26
RT Ponting/Aus	34/31	1154	5	46.16
SR Tendulkar/Ind	21/21	1141	1	57.05
AC Gilchrist/Aus	31/30	1098	1	37.86
ML Hayden/Aus	32/31	1037	5	39.88
CH Gayle/WI	21/21	981	2	51.63
Yasir Hameed/Pak	19/19	898	1	49.89
BC Lara/WI	21/21	888	2	46.74
DR Martyn/Aus	26/23	878	8	58.53
V Sehwag/Ind	27/27	871	0	32.26
M Trescothick/Eng	25/25	867	2	37.70

— PAIRED UP —

Every opening bat relies on an understanding of – and with – his partner, and Marcus Trescothick has been fortunate to have Michael Vaughan and Andrew Strauss as top-order soul mates. With Vaughan he scored a partnership total of 2,386 runs in 52 innings, an average of 48.7, while with Strauss he has produced partnerships totalling 1,124 across 18 innings (one of which was the formality of an unbeaten 4 in the 2004 fourth Test against the West Indies).

Overall, that's an average of 66.1, up to and including the second Test against South Africa at Durban in December 2004. That was the one, you might recall, in which the pair took England to 273 for 0 in the second innings – the fifth-best opening stand in the country's Test history – after the tourists were all out for 139 in the first. That effort allowed England to set a target of 378 and, but for bad light, could well have extended the side's winning streak to nine matches.

The figures for Trescothick–Strauss, Inc, from its birth at Lord's in May 2004 until the end of that year are shown below. The pair's first-innings performances are particularly strong, with partnerships averaging 74.88. That drops on second-innings scores to 56.25, although wearing pitches probably take much of the blame.

TRESCOTHICK–STRAUSS PARTNERSHIP TEST MATCHES, 2004

Test	First Innings	Second Innings
First v NZ (Home)	190	18
Second v NZ (Home)	153	18
Third v NZ (Home)	1	12
First v WI (Home)	29	86
Second v WI (Home)	77	24
Third v WI (Home)	0	15
Fourth v WI (Home)	51	4–0
First v SA (Away)	152	0
Second v SA (Away)	21	273

Impressive though this might seem, it's some way off the partnership average posted by South Africans Graeme Smith and Herschelle Gibbs. In 37 innings up to 2004, this pair scored 2,595 runs, at an average of 76.3. However, that 273 at Durban elevated Marcus and Andrew to the pantheon of true greats. For England, only Hobbs and Sutcliffe have done a better job. Enough said.

PARTNERS	INNINGS	PARTNERSHIP RUNS	AVERAGE
Hobbs/Sutcliffe	38	3,249	87.8
Trescothick/Strauss	18	1,124	66.1
Cowdrey/Pullar	15	906	64.7
Hobbs/Rhodes	36	2,146	61.3
Hutton/Washbrook	51	2,880	60.0
Gooch/Atherton	44	2,501	56.8

— CHANCE GONE —

Andrew Strauss appears to be one of those cricketers born to play Test matches. When called up by England to replace an injured Michael Vaughan in May 2004, he grabbed his chance with alacrity, securing a win at Lord's through a century and a 190 opening stand with Marcus Trescothick. Once picked, he turned in a string of top-class performances, worked hard for the team and proved a superb ambassador for his sport.

Not all England debuts have gone quite so smoothly. In May 1935 Oxford student Norman 'Mandy' Mitchell-Innes was picked for England on the strength of his stylish 168 against the touring South Africans at the Parks. He scored a humble five in his first innings and didn't bat in the second. Mandy (don't ask) then ruled himself out of the next Test by complaining of hay fever, an allergy that dogged his entire cricketing career. He suggested his landlord, Errol Holmes, as a replacement, but then lost a stack of brownie points by promptly nipping down to The Oval to hit 132 for Oxford University against Surrey. Lord's was unimpressed. Mandy never played Test cricket again.

— AWKWARD SPACE —

This is not a joke book (depending on your understanding of the term), but in order to fill an awkward space on this page We couldn't resist the following dressing-room favourite. What's the difference between a former England cricket captain and a driver who taps out phone messages while at the wheel? One's a Ted Dexter, the other's a Dead Texter. Oh, never mind.

— ANNUAL RETURN —

England fast bowler Steve Harmison almost lived to regret the long lay-off between the ICC Champions' Trophy final in September 2004 and England's first Test against South Africa at Port Elizabeth three months later. A rusty-looking Harmy returned 1–142 against the Proteas in that match – his worst ever Test performance – leaving him an agonising five short of the best total haul in a calendar year by an England bowler. Fortunately, he came good in the drawn second Test at Durban, bagging the five required.

MOST TEST WICKETS IN A CALENDAR YEAR (ENGLAND BOWLERS)

BOWLER	WICKETS	YEAR	NUMBER OF MATCHES
S Harmison	67	2004	13
IT Botham	66	1978	12
IT Botham	62	1981	13
SF Barnes	61	1912	9
A Fraser	58	1998	14

— PROMISED LAND —

'Diplomatic vacuum' is the technical Foreign Office term for unmitigated suspicion and loathing between two parties. If relations between British ministers and the ICC are anything to go by, English cricket is going to be gasping for air well into the 21st century.

It wasn't just the Zimbabwe tour fiasco, shambolic though that was. Earlier in 2004, the ICC's hopes for tax breaks on its annual £100 million income were dashed by the Treasury, despite the best efforts of UK Sport. The latter had hoped that tax concessions would persuade the ICC to remain at Lord's rather than up sticks to Ireland, Switzerland, Malaysia or Dubai.

Still fuming at this news, ICC chiefs then read comments by British Sports Minister Richard Caborn to the effect that he would 'like to meet the ICC when they are next in town'. Council president Ehsan Mani's response was understandably withering. 'The ICC have been "in town" since 1909,' he said. 'Our chief executive, Malcolm Speed, is based at Lord's and I live here.' Whatever happened to British diplomacy?

— PERCY'S PLUCKS —

In all the furore surrounding England's record-breaking winning streak, it's worth remembering the skipper from whom Michael Vaughan claimed the record. At Adelaide in February 1929, Percy Chapman managed his seventh win on the trot, a feat which began the previous summer with three Tests against a dreadful West Indies side making its entry into international cricket.

Chapman was a clubbable, carefree chap who enjoyed a stout in the lunch interval and shared Vaughan's team-building sentiments. He wasn't in the same league as his key batsmen – Hobbs, Hammond and Sutcliffe – but was a brilliant fielder, agile in spite of his size. In the first Ashes Test of 1929, he plucked out a remarkable catch at gully to see off Woodfull for a duck, then produced an even better effort to dismiss Bradman for one in the second innings.

The story goes that, as Bradman walked off, an incredulous Sir James Barrie, author of *Peter Pan*, turned to his friend Neville Cardus in the Brisbane crowd and asked, 'What evidence have we that the ball which Chapman threw up in the air is the same ball which left Bradman's bat?' For once, Cardus was reduced to goldfish impressions.

— CABLE TALK —

Cardus – or Sir Neville, as he later became – was a giant of 20th-century cricket journalism who dreaded the prospect of sub-editors mangling his copy. He particularly loathed punctuation errors and in despatches would spell out marks such as 'comma' and 'semi-colon' in full to ensure that they were properly inserted.

This did not, however, impress one exasperated editor who knew that Telegraph companies charged for every word. Concerned about Cardus's profligacy, he sent him a message which read, 'Please send story. We'll fix punctuation.' Sir Neville's response to such miserliness was suitably cutting. 'I'll send punctuation,' he cabled. 'You fill in words.'

— RUN KINGS —

Now here's a statistic you never thought you'd read. In 2004 the team with the best scoring rate (ie runs per over) in Test cricket was Michael Vaughan's England, with 3.55.* Even more astonishingly, Australia were pipped to second place by the West Indies. Here's a full breakdown for the big eight Test-playing nations as at December 2004:

England..3.55
West Indies..3.51
Australia..3.48
India..3.32
Sri Lanka...3.28
Pakistan...3.25
New Zealand 3.11
South Africa 3.03

— LEG THEORY —

Protection for batsmen facing quick bowling is now better than ever, but back in the 19th century players who dared to wear new-fangled leg guards were seen as softies by traditionalists. The president of MCC, the Reverend Lord Frederick Beauclerk, was a champion of this view...until he saw what a cricket ball could do to unprotected flesh.

Beauclerk's road-to-Damascus conversion occurred during a game organised by MCC at Leicester in August 1836 in which the North played the South. The event was a big commercial success, not least because the two fastest bowlers in the land – Alfred Mynn and Samuel Redgate – were lined up on opposing sides. Mynn, the son of a Kent gentleman farmer, delivered the ball with a speed and elegance that belied his 18-stone frame. (He once scolded a young cricketer he caught drinking tea, advising that 'beef and beer are the thing to play cricket on'.) Redgate was marginally slower, although in the previous year he had made his name by twice dismissing the gloriously named Fuller Pilch – considered the leading batsman of the age – for a duck in the Players versus Gentlemen match.

* To the first Test vs South Africa

Things didn't start too well for the South when Mynn – also a handy batsman – was struck on the ankle during the warm-up. He missed the first day's play, but his team-mates managed pretty well without him, reducing the North to 97–6 by the close. Mynn batted with a runner the following day, ending unbeaten on 21, but the effort aggravated his swollen leg, and when the North began their second innings he was again quite unable to bowl. By the third day he was telling his skipper that he'd bat only if required.

Inevitably, he *was* required. He limped to the wicket to face Redgate and batted doggedly to post a century. However, it cost him dear. With limited foot movement, he had to endure strike after strike against unprotected legs, a battery which only added to the painful inflammation. When the last wicket fell he limped off, undefeated, on 125.

Mynn staggered into a tent, beckoning Lord Beauclerk to attend him urgently. The MCC president was aghast at the state of his man's legs and immediately summoned a stagecoach to get him to London and expert medical assistance. This must have been a truly horrendous journey for Mynn, who, in his incapacitated state, found it impossible to climb inside. He was eventually manhandled onto the roof to endure 100-odd miles of rocking and rolling over the potholes of Watling Street.

Mynn insisted on beginning his recovery with a snifter or two at the Angel Tavern in St Martin's Lane, and by the time he was carried into St Bartholomew's Hospital his leg was in a truly parlous state. Leading surgeons seriously considered amputation, but the scalpel-happy among them were persuaded otherwise and Mynn eventually made a full recovery. The real lesson of his ordeal was that only fools refused leg guards against genuinely quick bowling. Beauclerk was certainly convinced, and by the time of WG Grace guards were standard equipment in the first-class game. According to one (unlikely) account, Grace actually wore Mynn's old leg guards when he scored 400 for the United South XI against a Grimsby XXII in 1876.

— INDEX —

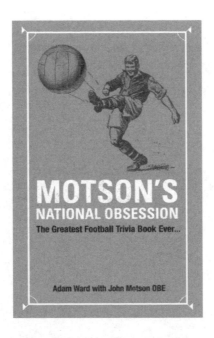

MOTSON'S NATIONAL OBSESSION
The Greatest Football Trivia Book Ever...
Adam Ward with John Motson OBE

1 86074 601 2 | £9.99

BEAUMONT'S UP AND UNDER
Trivial Delights from the World of Rugby Union
Bill Beaumont OBE with Mark Baldwin

1 86074 624 1 | £9.99

ALLISS' 19TH HOLE
Trivial Delights from the World of Golf
Peter Alliss with Rab MacWilliam

1 86074 623 3 | £9.99